THE MAKING OF
THE EUROPEAN AGE

THE ILLUSTRATED
HISTORY OF THE WORLD

VOLUME 6

THE MAKING OF
THE EUROPEAN AGE

J. M. ROBERTS

New York
Oxford University Press

The Illustrated History of the World

This edition first published in 1999 in the United States of America by
Oxford University Press, Inc.,
198 Madison Avenue, New York, N.Y. 10016
Oxford is a registered trademark of Oxford University Press

THE MAKING OF THE EUROPEAN AGE
Copyright © Editorial Debate SA 1998
Text Copyright © J. M. Roberts 1976, 1980, 1983, 1987, 1988, 1992, 1998
Artwork and Diagrams Copyright © Editorial Debate SA 1998
(for copyright of photographs and maps, see acknowledgments on page 192, which are
to be regarded as an extension of this copyright)

Art Direction by Duncan Baird Publishers
Produced by Duncan Baird Publishers, London, England,
and Editorial Debate, Madrid, Spain

Series ISBN 0-19-521529-X
Volume ISBN 0-19-521524-9

DBP staff:
Senior editor: Joanne Levêque
Assistant editor: Georgina Harris
Senior designer: Steven Painter
Assistant designer: Anita Schnable
Picture research: Julia Ruxton
Sales fulfilment: Ian Smalley
Map artwork: Russell Bell
Decorative borders: Lorraine Harrison

Editorial Debate staff:
Editors and picture researchers:
Isabel Belmonte Martínez, Feliciano Novoa Portela,
Ruth Betegón Díez, Dolores Redondo
Editorial coordination: Ana Lucía Vila

Typeset in Sabon 11/15 pt
Color reproduction by Trescan, Madrid, Spain
Printed in Singapore by Imago Limited

NOTE
The abbreviations CE and BCE are used throughout this book:
CE Common Era (the equivalent of AD)
BCE Before Common Era (the equivalent of BC)

10 9 8 7 6 5 4 3 2 1

CONTENTS

THE MAKING OF THE EUROPEAN AGE

AFTER 1500 OR SO, there are many signs that a new age of world history is beginning. Some of them have already appeared in these pages; the discoveries in the Americas and the first shoots of European enterprise in Asia are among them. At the outset they provide hints about the dual nature of a new age – that it is increasingly an age of truly world history and that it is one whose story is dominated by the astonishing success of one civilization among many, that of Europe. These are two aspects of the same process; there is a more and more continuous and organic inter-connexion between events in all countries, but it is largely to be explained by the efforts of Europeans. They eventually became masters of the globe and they used their mastery – sometimes without knowing it – to make the world one. As a result world history has for the last two or three centuries a growing identity and unity of theme.

In a famous passage, the English historian Macaulay once spoke of red men scalping one another on the shores of the Great Lakes so that a European king could rob his neighbour of a province he coveted. This was one striking side of the story we must now embark upon – the gradual entanglement of struggles the world over with one another in greater and greater wars – but politics, empire-building and military expansion were only a tiny part of what was going on. The economic integration of the globe was another part of the process; more important still was the spreading of common assumptions and ideas. The result was to be, in a cant phrase of today, "One World" – of sorts. The age of independent or nearly independent civilizations has come to a close.

Men and nations are still so different from one another that this may seem at first sight a wildly mislead-ing exaggeration. National, cultural and racial differences have not ceased to produce and inspire appalling conflicts; the history of the centuries since 1500 can be (and often is) written mainly as a series of wars and violent struggles and men in different countries obviously do not feel much more like one another than did their predecessors centuries ago. Yet they are much more alike than their ancestors of, say, the tenth century and show it in hundreds of ways ranging from the superficialities of dress to the forms in which they get their living and organize their societies. The origins, extent and limits of this change make up most of the story which follows. It is the outcome of something still going on in many places which we sometimes call modernization. For centuries it has been grinding away at differences between cultures and it is the deepest and most fundamental expression of the growing integration of world history. Another way of describing the process is to say that the world is Europeanized, for modernization is above all a matter of ideas and techniques which are European in origin. Whether "modernization" is the same as "Europeanization", though, can be left for discussion elsewhere; perhaps it is only a matter of verbal preferences. What is obvious is that, chronologically, it is with the modernization of Europe that the unification of world history begins. A great change in Europe was the starting-point of modern history.

Europe seated on her throne, on the cover of *Theatrum Orbis Terrarum*, a book produced in Antwerp in 1572, holds both a sceptre, representing world power, and an orb decorated with a crucifix, representing Christianity. Europe clearly dominates the three other feminine figures at her feet: these symbolize Asia, in elaborate dress; Africa, who is half naked; and America, who, entirely naked, brandishes a human head as a sign of her cannibalism, which was encountered in Brazil and elsewhere in the 16th century.

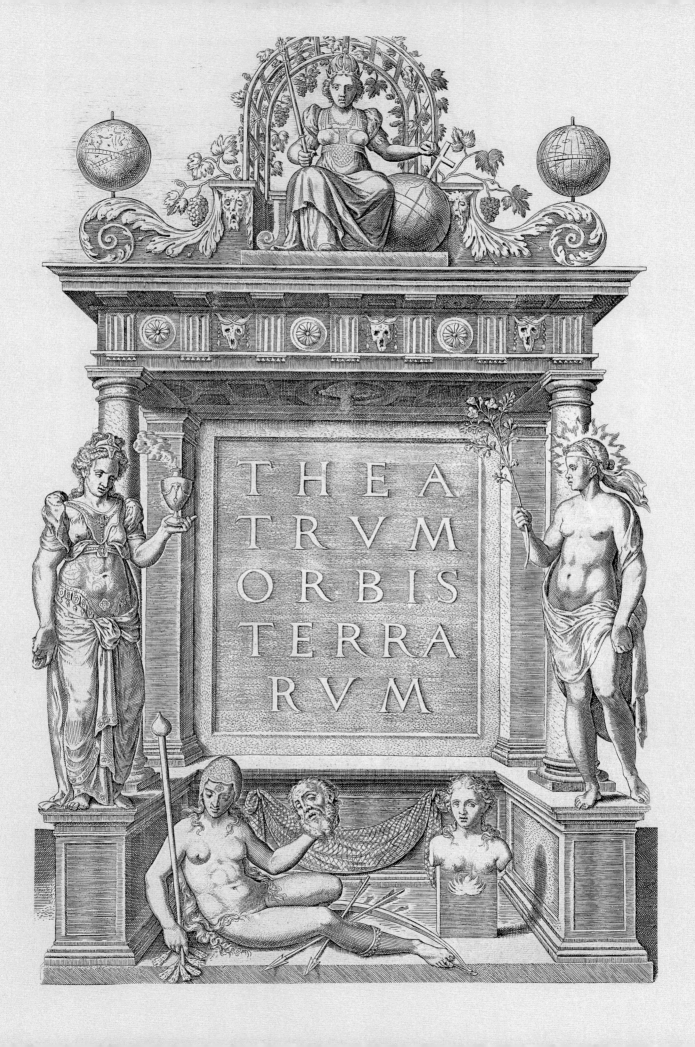

THEA
TRVM
ORBIS
TERRA
RVM

1 A NEW KIND OF SOCIETY: EARLY MODERN EUROPE

THE TERM "modern history" is a familiar one, but it does not always mean the same thing. There was a time when modern history was what had happened since the "ancient" history whose subject-matter was the story of the Jews, Greeks and Romans; this is a sense which, for example, is still used to define a course of study at Oxford which includes the Middle Ages. Then it came to be distinguished from "medieval" history, too. Now a further refinement is often made, for historians have begun to make distinctions within it and sometimes speak of an "early modern" period. By this, though, they are really drawing our attention to a process, for they apply it to the era in which the modern Atlantic world emerged from the tradition-dominated, agrarian, superstitious and confined western Christendom of the Middle Ages, and this took place at different times in different countries. In England it happened very rapidly; in Spain it was far from complete by 1800, while much of eastern Europe was still hardly affected by it even a century later. But the reality of the process is obvious, for all the irregularity with which it expressed itself. So is its importance, for it laid the groundwork for a European world hegemony.

A useful starting-point for thinking about what was involved is to begin with the simple and obvious truth that for most of human history most people's lives have been deeply and cruelly shaped by the fact that they have had little or no choice about the way in which they could provide themselves and their families with shelter and enough to eat. The possibility that things might be otherwise has only recently become a conceivable one to even a minority of the world's population and it became a reality for any substantial number of people only with changes in the economy of early modern Europe, for the most part, west of the Elbe.

AN AGE OF MEASUREMENT

WE CAN FOLLOW SOME of these economic changes as we can follow no earlier ones because, for the first time, there is reasonably plentiful and continuous

This metal calculating machine was built by the French mathematician, physicist, writer and theologian Blaise Pascal (1623–1662) and was patented in 1647. He invented the machine in order to assist his father with his accountancy work.

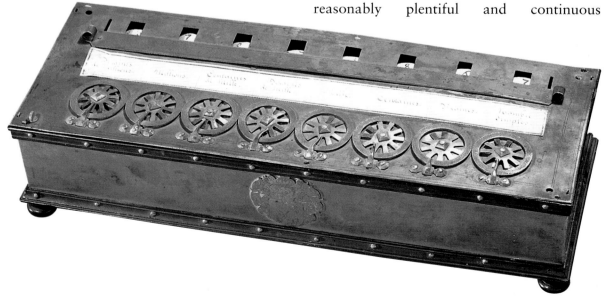

quantified data. In one important respect, historical evidence gets much more informative in the last four or five centuries: it becomes much more statistical. Measurement therefore becomes easier. The source of new statistical material was often government. For many reasons, governments wanted to know more and more about the resources or potential resources at their disposal. But private records, especially of business, also give us much more numerical data after 1500. The multiplication of copies as paper and printing became more common meant that the chance of their survival was enormously increased. Commercial techniques appeared which required publication of data in collated forms; the movements of ships, or reports of prices, for example. Moreover, as historians have refined their techniques, they have attacked even poor or fragmentary sources with much greater success than was possible even a few years ago.

THE LIMITATIONS OF STATISTICAL EVIDENCE

All this data has provided much knowledge of the size and shape of change in early modern Europe, though we must be careful not to exaggerate either the degree of precision such material permits or what can be learnt from it. For a long time the collection of good statistics was very difficult. Even quite elementary questions, about, for example, who lived in a certain place, were very difficult to answer accurately until recent times. One of the great aims of reforming monarchs in the eighteenth century was merely to carry out accurate listings of land within their states, cadastral surveys, as they were called, or even to find out how many subjects they had. It was only in 1801 that the first census was held in Great Britain – nearly eight

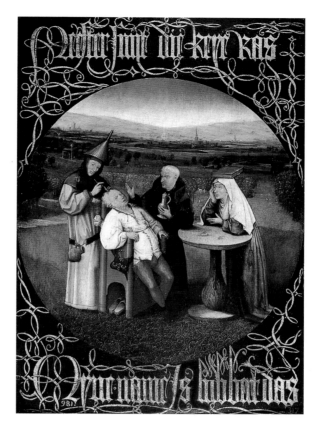

This painting by the Dutch artist Hieronymus Bosch (c.1453–1516), entitled *The Extraction of the Stone of Madness*, caricatures the co-existence of superstition, faith, knowledge and primitive surgery in 15th-century society.

centuries after the Domesday Book. France did not have her first official census until 1876 nor the Russian Empire her only one until 1897. Such delays are not really surprising. A census or a survey requires a complex and reliable administrative machine. It may arouse strong opposition (when governments seek new information, new taxes often follow). Such difficulties are enormously increased where the population is as illiterate as it was in much of Europe for the greater part of modern history.

New statistical material can also raise as many historical problems as it solves. It can reveal a bewildering variety of contemporary phenomena which often makes generalization harder; it has become much harder to say anything at all about the French peasantry of the eighteenth century since research revealed the diversity hidden by that simple term and that perhaps there was no such thing as *a* French peasantry, but only several different

Demographic growth

The lack of any reliable population census during most of this period – the few surveys that were carried out at the beginning of the 18th century were estimations for economic or military use – has meant that records of births and deaths in local parish registers are the principal source of evidence for historians studying the demography of the early modern era. Population growth had been moderate and irregular in the 16th and 17th centuries. However, in spite of short life expectancy, later marriages and a high rate of infant mortality, there can be no doubt that the rate of growth of the European population in the second half of the 18th century began to quicken.

This was due to several factors. By the mid-18th century, improved farming and husbandry meant that nutrition was better and fewer people were dying of hunger. Transport facilities, which played an important role in grain distribution, had also improved.

From the middle of the 16th century, and partly because of the interest of the Renaissance painters, numerous illustrated books on anatomy were published, which helped to improve medical knowledge. By the end of the 17th century, clear descriptions of the symptoms of diseases such as rickets, diabetes, gout and tuberculosis were available, and the circulation of the blood had been discovered. But only very few people were treated by qualified doctors. The peasant masses continued to rely on local "quacks" or travelling practitioners.

The last epidemic of the plague struck in 1713, after which it became a local phenomenon. Growing experience in the use of preventative measures to avoid contagion (vigilance at the ports, and the introduction of quarantine and sanitary cordons) had helped to achieve this. However, typhoid, smallpox, tuberculosis, diphtheria and malaria continued to wreak havoc.

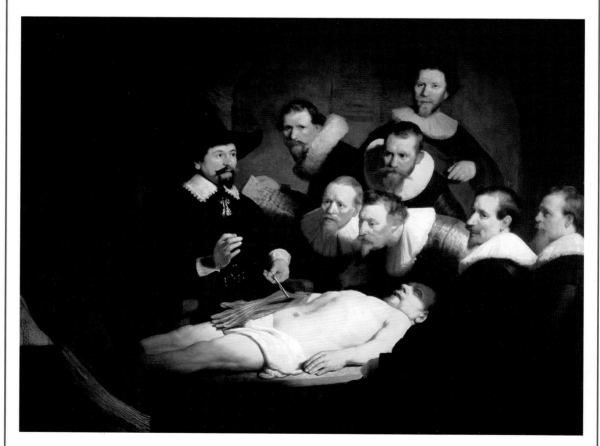

The Anatomy Lesson, *painted in 1632 by the Dutch artist Rembrandt (1606–1669). Anatomical research led to medical advances which, in turn, eventually contributed to an increased life expectancy in Europe.*

The French artist Louis Le Nain (c.1593–1648) and his brothers Antoine (c.1588–1648) and Matthieu (c.1607–1677) painted numerous scenes depicting peasant life. Works such as *Peasant Family at Home* provide an insight into the living conditions of rural workers in 17th-century Europe.

ones. Finally, too, statistics can illuminate facts while throwing no light at all on causes. Nevertheless after 1500 we are more and more in an age of measurement and the overall effect of this is to make it easier to make defensible statements about what was happening than in earlier times at other places.

POPULATION TRENDS IN EUROPE

DEMOGRAPHIC HISTORY is the most obvious example of a subject that we are able to discuss with more certainty. At the end of the fifteenth century European population was poised on the edge of growth which has gone on ever since. After 1500 we may crudely distinguish two phases. Until about the middle of the eighteenth century the increase of population was (except for notable local and temporary interruptions) relatively slow and steady; this roughly corresponds to "early modern" history and was

The population of Europe 1500–1800

Demographic growth of around 40 per cent occurred in Europe between 1500 and 1700, although during the 17th century there was a negative demographic balance in Spain, several regions of southern Italy and central Germany. This overall growth was less than half of that which was to take place during the 18th century. The estimated population of various European countries during this period is shown in millions in this chart.

	1500	1600	1700	1800
Spain and Portugal	9.3	11.3	10	14.6
Italy	10.5	13.3	13.3	18.1
France (inc. Lorraine and Savoy)	16.4	18.5	21	26.9
Benelux countries	1.9	2.9	3.4	5.2
British Isles	4.4	6.8	9.3	15.9
Scandinavian countries	1.5	2.4	2.8	3.2
Germany	12	15	15	24.5
Switzerland	0.8	1	1.2	1.8
Russia	9	15.5	17.5	
Total for Europe	65.8	86.7	92.5	110.2 (without Russia)

one of the things characterizing it. In the second phase the increase much accelerated and great changes followed. Only the first phase concerns us here, because it regulated the way in which modern Europe took shape. The general facts and trends within it are clear enough. Though they rely heavily on estimates, the figures are much better based than in earlier times, in part because there was almost continuous interest in population problems from the early seventeenth century onwards. This contributed to the foundation of the science of statistics (then called "Political Arithmetic") at the end of the seventeenth century, mainly by the English. They did some remarkable work, though their efforts only provided a tiny island of relatively rigorous method in a sea of guesses and inferences. Nevertheless the broad picture is clear. In 1500 Europe had about eighty million inhabitants, two centuries later she had less than one hundred and fifty million and in 1800 slightly less than two hundred million. Before 1750 Europe had grown fairly

steadily at a rate which maintained her share of the world's population at about one-fifth until 1700 or so, but by 1800 she had nearly a quarter of the world's inhabitants.

THE BIRTH-RATE AND LIFE EXPECTANCY

For a long time, obviously, there were no such startling disparities as appeared later between the rate of growth in Europe and that elsewhere. It seems reasonable to conclude that this meant that in other ways, too, European and non-European populations were less different than they were to come to be after 1800. The usual age of death among Europeans, for example, still remained low. Before 1800 they were on the average always much younger than nowadays, because people died earlier. At birth a French peasant of the eighteenth century had a life expectancy of about twenty-two years and only a roughly one-in-four chance of surviving infancy. His chances were therefore much the same as those of an Indian peasant in 1950 or an Italian under imperial Rome. Comparatively few people would have survived their forties, and, since they were less well fed than we are, they would have looked old to us at that age, and probably rather small in stature and unhealthy-looking. As in the Middle Ages, women tended still to die before men. This meant that many men made a second or even a third marriage, not, as today, because of divorce, but because they were soon widowers. The average European couple had a fairly short married life. West of a line running roughly from the Baltic to the Adriatic, they had shorter marriages than east of it, moreover, because those who lived there tended to make their first marriage later in their twenties, and this was long to be a habit making for different population patterns east

Diagram by Mallet and Malthus

Research carried out by the Swiss doctor E Mallet in Geneva and by the English economist Thomas Malthus (1766–1834) produced slightly different figures for life expectancy during the mid-16th to 18th centuries, as shown in these charts. Short life expectancy is linked to a high mortality rate among women and children, owing to a general lack of hygiene and poor sanitary conditions and nutrition, as well as to natural or human disasters.

Average life span		
	Mallet	Malthus
Mid-16th century	21 years, 2 months	18 years, 6 months
17th century	25 years, 8 months	23 years, 4 months
18th century	32 years, 9 months	32 years, 3 months

Life expectancy at birth		
	Mallet	Malthus
Mid-16th century	8 years, 7 months	4 years, 10 months
17th century	13 years, 3 months	11 years, 7 months
18th century	27 years, 9 months	27 years, 2 months

and west. Generally, though, if Europeans were well-off they could afford a fairly large family; the poor had smaller ones. There is strong inferential evidence both that some form of family limitation was already taking place in some places in the seventeenth century and that other methods of achieving it than abortion and infanticide were available and widely known. No doubt both cultural and economic facts are needed to explain this mysterious topic. It remains one of those areas where a largely illiterate society is almost impossible to penetrate historically. We can say very little with confidence about the material facts of early birth control and still less about its implications – if there were any – for the ways in which early modern Europeans thought about themselves and their control over their own lives.

TOWNS AND CITIES

OVERALL THE DEMOGRAPHIC FACTS reflect the continuing economic predominance of agriculture. For a long time it produced only slightly more food than was needed and could only feed a slowly growing population. In 1500 Europe was still largely a rural continent of villages in which people lived at a pretty low level of subsistence. It would have seemed very empty to modern eyes. England's population, heavy in relation to area by comparison with the rest of the continent, was in 1800 only about a fifth of today's; in eastern Europe there were huge empty spaces for which population was eagerly sought by rulers who encouraged immigration in all sorts of ways. Yet the towns and cities managed to grow in number and size, one or two of them spectacularly faster than the population as a whole. Amsterdam reached a total of about 200,000 inhabitants in the eighteenth century. Paris

Urbanization in Europe

The growth of European cities resulted partly from the expansion of traditional activities and partly from the development of new functions. Towns thrived around ports, markets, manufacturing or mining centres and the headquarters of secular government or church dignitaries. After 1600, trade and banking centres also attracted ever-increasing populations. Spa towns began to appear and larger fortified towns were founded, as were new naval bases.

However, the size of urban centres was very different from that of modern cities. In around 1600 only about 5 per cent of the total population lived in cities with between 20,000 and 30,000 inhabitants. Of every ten Europeans, seven lived in the rural areas and two in small country towns.

The distribution of urban centres on the European map was very unbalanced, with the highest concentration of towns to be found on the coastal plains of the North Sea.

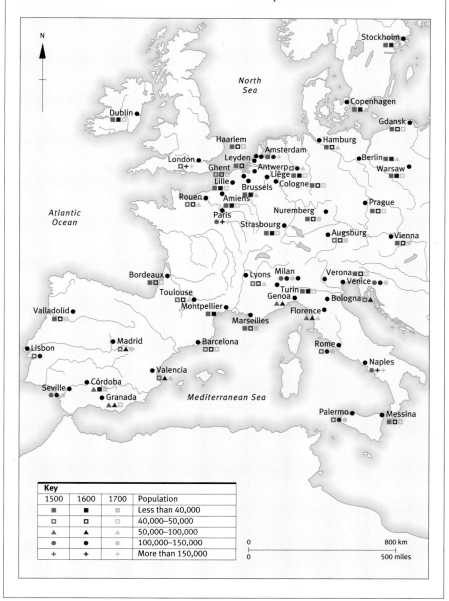

Key			
1500	1600	1700	Population
■	■	■	Less than 40,000
□	□	□	40,000–50,000
▲	▲	▲	50,000–100,000
●	●	●	100,000–150,000
+	+	+	More than 150,000

probably doubled in size between 1500 and 1700, and rose to slightly less than a half-million. London shot ahead of Paris by going up from about 120,000 to nearly 700,000 in the same two centuries; in a much smaller English population this, of course, meant a much bigger shift to urban life. A significant new word came into use in English: suburbs. But it is not easy to generalize about medium-sized and smaller towns. Most were quite small, still under 20,000 in 1700, but the nine European cities of more than 100,000 in 1500 had become at least a dozen two hundred years later. Yet Europe's predominance in urbanization was not so marked in these centuries as it was to become and there were still many great cities in other continents. The city of Mexico, for example, outdid all European cities of the sixteenth century with its population of 300,000.

DIFFERENTIATION IN EUROPEAN GROWTH

Neither urbanization nor population growth was evenly spread. France remained the largest west European nation in these years;

she had about 21 million inhabitants in 1700, when England and Wales had only about 6 million. But it is not easy to make comparisons because estimates are much less reliable for some areas than others and because boundary changes often make it hard to be sure what we are talking about under the same name at different times. Some certainly underwent checks and possibly setbacks in their population growth in a wave of seventeenth-century disasters. Spain, Italy and Germany all had bad outbreaks of epidemic disease in the 1630s and there were other celebrated local attacks such as the Great Plague of London of 1665. Famine was another sporadic and local check; we hear even of cannibalism in the middle seventeenth century in Germany. Poor feeding and the lower resistance it led to quickly produced disaster when coupled to the disruption of the economy which could follow a bad harvest. When accentuated by warfare, of which there was always a great deal in central Europe, the result could be cataclysmic. Famine and the diseases which followed armies about in their baggage-trains could quickly depopulate a small area. Yet this in part reflected the degree to which economic life was still localized; the

The Italian city-states were the most dynamic in the Mediterranean in the 16th century. They were thriving trade and industrial centres and had commercial ties with both the Near East and western Europe. Known as the *Carta della Catena,* this view of the city of Florence dates from 1480.

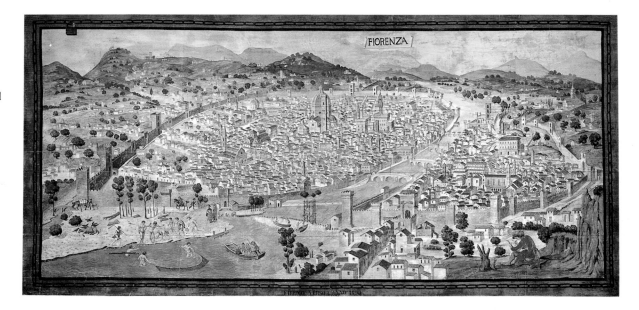

For most 16th-century Europeans, the great religious festivals and the seasonal agrarian tasks, with their cyclical rhythms, served to mark the passing of time. One of the most important activities of the year is depicted in this painting, *Hay Making in July*, by Pieter Brueghel the Elder (c.1520–1569).

converse was that a particular town might get off unscathed even in a campaigning zone if it escaped siege or sack, while only a few miles away another was devastated. The situation was always precarious until population growth began to be overtaken by productivity.

AGRICULTURAL ADVANCES

IN PRODUCTIVITY LEVELS, as in so many things, different countries have different histories. A renewed expansion of agriculture seems to have got under way in the middle of the fifteenth century. One sign was the resumption of land which had reverted to waste in the depopulation of the fourteenth century. Yet this had made little headway in any but a few places before 1550 or so. It remained confined to them for a long time,

An August corn harvest is depicted in this engraving from a French Book of Hours (c.1520). At harvest-time, debts were settled, exchanges were made at markets and fairs, taxes were paid and preparations were made for winter. If the harvest failed, however, disaster inevitably followed.

though by then there had already been important improvements in techniques which raised the productivity of land, mainly by the application of labour, that is by intensive cultivation. Where their impact was not felt the medieval past long lingered in the countryside. Even the coming of money was slow in breaking into the near self-sufficiency of some communities. In eastern Europe serfdom actually extended its range when it was dying out elsewhere. Yet by 1800, taking Europe as a whole and a few leading countries in particular, agriculture was one of the two economic sectors where progress was most marked (commerce was the other). Overall, it had proved capable of sustaining a continuing rise of population at first very slowly, but at a quickening rate.

Agricultural progress increasingly took two main forms: orientation towards the market, and technical innovation. They were interconnected. A large population in the neighbourhood meant a market and therefore an incentive. Even in the fifteenth century the inhabitants of the Low Countries were already leaders in the techniques of intensive cultivation. It was in Flanders, too, that better drainage opened the way to better pasture and to a larger animal population. Another area with relatively large town populations was the Po valley; in north Italy new crops were introduced into Europe from Asia. Rice, for example, an important addition to the European larder, appeared in the Arno and Po valleys in the fifteenth century. On the other hand not all crops enjoyed instant success. It took about two centuries for the potato, which came to Europe from America, to become established as a normal item of consumption in England, Germany and France, in spite of its obvious nutritional value and much promotional folklore stressing its qualities as an aphrodisiac and value in the treatment of warts.

ENGLISH AGRICULTURAL PROWESS

From the Low Countries agricultural improvements spread in the sixteenth century to eastern England where they were slowly elaborated further. In the seventeenth century London became a corn-exporting port and in the next other Europeans came to England to learn how to farm. The eighteenth century also brought better husbandry and animal breeding. Such improvements led to yields on crops and a quality of livestock now taken for granted but until then unimaginable. The appearance of the countryside and its occupants was transformed. Agriculture provided the first demonstration of what might be done by even rudimentary science – by experiment, observation, record, and experiment again – to increase human beings'

The Europe of this time was a rural continent; the majority of its population lived in the countryside and most economic activity was related to working the land. Farm labourers are shown working and resting in the fields during the wheat harvest in this 16th-century manuscript illustration.

This portrait by Thomas Gainsborough (1727–1788), entitled *Mr and Mrs Andrews*, was painted in 1748 and reflects the subjects' wealth and social position. Behind the rich landowner and his wife lie rows of neat enclosed fields – the product of the steady transformation of English agricultural methods.

control of their environment more rapidly than could the selection imposed by custom. Improvement favoured the reorganization of land in bigger farms, the reduction of the number of smallholders except on land which specially favoured them, the employment of wage-labour, and high capital investment in buildings, drainage and machinery. The speed of change must not be exaggerated. One index of change in England was the pace of "enclosure", the consolidation for private use of the open fields and common lands of the traditional village. It was only at the end of the eighteenth century and the beginning of the nineteenth that the Acts of Parliament authorizing this became frequent and numerous. The complete integration of agriculture with the market economy and the treatment of land simply as a commodity like any other would have to wait for the nineteenth century, even in England, the leader of world agriculture until the opening of the overseas cornlands. Yet by the eighteenth century the way ahead was beginning to appear.

THE RETREAT OF FAMINE

Overall agricultural change in the end eliminated the recurrent dearths which so long retained their power to destroy demographic advance. Perhaps the last moment when European population seems to have pressed on resources so as to threaten another great calamity like that of the fourteenth century came at the end of the sixteenth century. In the next bad spell, in the middle decades of the following century, England and the Netherlands escaped the worst. Thereafter, famine and dearth become in Europe local and national events, still capable, it is true, of causing large-scale demographic damage, but gradually succumbing to the increasing availability of imported grain. Bad harvests, it has been said, made France "one great hospital" in 1708–9, but that was in wartime. Later in the century some Mediterranean countries depended for their flour on corn from the Baltic lands. True, it would be a long time before import would be a sure resource; often it could not operate quickly enough,

A plentiful meal, such as the one depicted in *The Wedding Feast* by the Flemish painter Pieter Brueghel the Elder (c.1520–1569), would have been a rare treat in the daily lives of most European peasants.

especially where land transport was required. Some parts of France and Germany were to suffer dearth even in the nineteenth century, and in the eighteenth century the French population grew faster than production so that the standard of living of many French people then actually fell back. For the English rural labourer, though, some of that century was later looked back to as a golden age of plentiful wheaten bread and even meat on the table.

EMIGRATION TO THE NEW WORLD

In the late sixteenth century one response to the obscurely felt pressure of an expanding population upon slowly growing resources had been the promoting of emigration. By 1800, Europeans had made a large contribution to the peopling of new lands overseas. Though far from so great a one as was to come, this has to be taken into account in their demographic history. In 1751 an American reckoned that North America contained a million persons of British origin; modern calculations are that about 250,000 British emigrants went to the New World in the seventeenth century, one and a half million in the next. There were also Germans (about 200,000) there, and French emigrants in Canada. By 1800 it seems reasonable to suppose that something like two million Europeans had gone to America north of the Rio Grande. South of it there were about 100,000 Spaniards and Portuguese.

THE NEW COMMERCIAL WORLD

F EAR THAT THERE WAS NOT ENOUGH to eat at home helped to initiate these great migrations and reflected the continuing pre-eminence of agriculture in all thinking about economic life. There were important changes in three centuries in the structure and scale of all the main sectors of the European economy, but it was still true in 1800 (as it had been true in 1500) that the agricultural sector predominated even in France and England, the two largest Western countries where commerce and manufacture had much progressed. Moreover, nowhere was anything but a tiny part of the population engaged in industry entirely unconnected with agriculture. Brewers, weavers, and dyers all depended on it, while many who grew crops or cultivated land also span, wove or dealt in commodities for the market. Apart from agriculture, it is only in the commercial sector that we can observe sweeping change. Here there is from the second half of the fifteenth century a visible quickening of tempo. Europe was regaining something like the commercial vigour first displayed in the thirteenth century. It showed in scale, technique and direction. Again there is a connexion with the

growth of towns. They both needed and provided a living for specialists. The great fairs and markets of the Middle Ages still continued. So did medieval laws on usury and the restrictive practices of guilds. Yet a whole new commercial world came into existence before 1800.

It was already discernible in the sixteenth century when there began the long expansion of world commerce which was to last, virtually uninterrupted except briefly by war, until 1930, and then to be resumed again after the next world war. It started by carrying further the shift of economic gravity from southern to northwestern Europe, from the Mediterranean to the Atlantic, which has already been remarked. One contribution to this was made by political troubles and wars such as ruined Italy in the early sixteenth century; others are comprised in tiny, short-lived but crucial pressures like the Portuguese harassment of Jews which led to so many of them going, with their commercial skills, to the Low Countries at about the same time.

In 17th-century England and France, the poor spent up to 80 per cent of their incomes on fresh foodstuffs. Although bartering was still predominant in some rural areas, perishable goods were increasingly bought and sold at weekly markets. This scene, depicting an open-air market in the Quai des Grands-Augustins in Paris, dates from c.1660.

The great commercial success story of the sixteenth century was Antwerp's, though it collapsed after a few decades in political and economic disaster. In the seventeenth century Amsterdam and London surpassed it. In each case an important trade based on a well-populated hinterland provided profits for diversification into manufacturing industry, services and banking. The old banking supremacy of the medieval Italian cities passed first to Flanders and the German bankers of the sixteenth century and then, finally, to Holland and London. The Bank of Amsterdam and the Bank of England were already international economic forces in the seventeenth century. About them clustered other banks and merchant houses undertaking operations of credit and finance. Interest rates came down and the bill of exchange, a medieval invention, underwent an enormous extension of use and became the primary financial instrument of international trade.

Money was used for an ever greater diversity of transactions by the 16th century. The amount of trade on credit increased as drafts, letters of credit and bills of exchange became acceptable. Many specialized dealers, such as those portrayed by Marinus van Reymerswaele in *The Money Changer and his Wife* (c.1540), flourished, and speculation and fraud were rife.

THE APPARATUS OF MODERN CAPITALISM

The growing importance of the bill of exchange marked the beginning of the increasing use of paper, instead of bullion. In the eighteenth century came the first European paper currencies and the invention of the cheque. Joint stock companies generated another form of negotiable security, their own shares. Quotation of these in London coffee-houses in the seventeenth century was overtaken by the foundation of the London Stock Exchange. By 1800 similar institutions existed in many other countries. New schemes for the mobilization of capital and its deployment proliferated in London, Paris and Amsterdam. Lotteries and tontines at one time enjoyed a vogue; so did some spectacularly disastrous investment projects, of which the most notorious was the great English South Sea "Bubble". But all the time the world was growing more commercial, more used to the idea of employing money to make money, and was supplying itself with the apparatus of modern capitalism.

One effect quickly appeared in the much greater attention paid to commercial questions in diplomatic negotiation from the later seventeenth century and in the fact that countries were prepared to fight over them. The English and Dutch went to war over trade in 1652. This opened a long era during which they, the French and the Spanish, fought again and again over quarrels in which questions of trade were important and often paramount.

Governments not only looked after their merchants by going to war to uphold their interests, but also intervened in other ways in the working of the commercial economy. One advantage they could offer was a grant of monopoly privileges to a company under a charter; this made the raising of capital easier by offering some security for a return. In the end people came to think that chartered companies might not be the best way of securing economic advantage and they fell into disfavour (enjoying a last brief revival at the end of the nineteenth century). None the less, such activities closely involved government and therefore the concerns of the business community shaped both policy and law.

THE FIRST COMMERCIAL LIFE INSURANCE

Occasionally the interplay of commercial development and society seems to throw light on changes with very deep implications indeed. One example came when a seventeenth-century English financier for the first time offered life insurance to the public. There had already begun the practice of

As the rate of wholesale trade increased and became more complex, representatives and intermediaries became more common, building up reputations based on their specialization, for the region in which they worked, or for the company to which they belonged. *Portrait of Gisze the Merchant* was painted by Hans Holbein the Younger (1497–1543).

selling annuities on an individual's life. What was new was the application of actuarial science and the newly available statistics of "political arithmetic" to this business. A reasonable calculation instead of a bet was now possible on a matter hitherto of awe-inspiring uncertainty and irrationality: death. With increasing refinement men would go on to offer (at a price) protection against a wide range of disaster. This would, incidentally, also provide another and very important device for the mobilization of wealth in large amounts for further investment. But the timing of the discovery of life insurance, at the start of what has sometimes been called the "Age of Reason", suggests also that the dimensions of economic change are sometimes very far-reaching indeed. It was one tiny source and expression of a coming secularizing of the universe.

INTERNATIONAL TRADE

THE MOST IMPRESSIVE structural development in European commerce was the sudden new importance to it of overseas trade from the second half of the seventeenth century onwards. This was part of the shift of economic activity from Mediterranean to northern Europe already observable before 1500. By the late seventeenth century, though the closed trade of Spain and Portugal with their transatlantic colonies was important, overseas commerce was dominated by the Dutch and their followers and increasingly successful rivals, the English. Dutch commerce grew out of the supply of salted herrings to European markets and the possession of a particularly suitable bulk-carrying vessel, the "flute" or "fly-boat". With this the Dutch dominated the important Baltic trade from whose mastery they advanced to become the carriers of Europe. In the later seventeenth century they tended to be displaced gradually by the English, though they maintained a wide spread of colonies and trading stations, especially in the Far East, where they had succeeded the Portuguese in the domination of maritime commerce. The Atlantic was the basis of English supremacy at sea. Fish was important here, too. The English caught the immensely nutritious and therefore immensely valuable cod on the Newfoundland banks, dried it and salted it ashore, and then sold it in Mediterranean countries, where fish was in great demand because of the practice of fasting on Fridays. *Bacalao*, as it was called, can still be found on the tables of Portugal and southern Spain,

The Atlantic coastal ports enjoyed a level of trade equal to that of the Baltic and the Mediterranean in variety and intensity, but were also the departure points for transoceanic trade – the most spectacular of the age. The port of Lisbon is portrayed in this 16th-century painting.

Together with Lisbon, the port of Seville, depicted in this painting, played a crucial role in the link between the Old and the New worlds. It was also a distribution centre for precious metals, which were dispersed from Seville throughout the rest of Europe and the world.

away from the tourist coast. Gradually, both Dutch and English broadened and diversified their carrying trade and became dealers themselves, too. Nor was France out of the race; her overseas trade doubled in the first half of the seventeenth century.

Rising populations and some assurance of adequate transport (water was always cheaper than land carriage) slowly built up an international trade in cereals. Shipbuilding itself promoted the movement of such commodities as pitch, flax or timber, staples first of Baltic trade and later important in the economy of North America. More than European consumption was involved; all this took place in a setting of growing colonial empires. By the eighteenth century we are already in the presence of an oceanic economy and an international trading community which does business – and fights and intrigues for it – around the globe.

BLACK SLAVERY

IN THE NEW GLOBAL ECONOMY an important and growing part was played by slaves. Most of them were black Africans, the first of whom to be brought to Europe were sold at Lisbon in 1444. In Europe itself, slavery had by then all but withered away (though Europeans were still being enslaved and sold into slavery by Arabs and Turks). Now it was to undergo a vast extension in other continents. Within two or three years over a thousand more blacks had been sold by the Portuguese, who soon set up a permanent slaving station in West Africa. Such figures show the rapid discovery of the profitability of the new traffic but gave little hint of the scale of what was to come. What was already clear was the brutality of the business (the Portuguese quickly noted that the seizure of children usually ensured the docile captivity of the parents) and the complicity of Africans in it; as the search for slaves went further inland, it became simpler to rely on local potentates who would round up captives and barter them wholesale.

For a long time, Europe and the Portuguese and Spanish settlements in the Atlantic islands took almost all the slaves West Africa supplied. Then came a change. From the mid-sixteenth century African slaves were shipped across the Atlantic to Brazil, the Caribbean islands and the North American mainland. The trade thus entered upon a long period of dramatic growth whose

demographic, economic and political consequences are still with us. African slaves are by no means the only ones important in modern history, nor were Europeans the only slavers. None the less, black slavery based on the buying of Africans from other Africans by Portuguese, Englishmen, Dutchmen and Frenchmen, and their sale to other Europeans in the Americas, is a phenomenon whose repercussions have been much more profound than the enslavement of Europeans by Ottomans or Africans by Arabs. Much of the labour which made American colonies possible and viable was supplied by black slaves, though for climatic reasons the slave population was not uniformly spread among them. Always the great majority of slaves worked in agriculture or domestic service: black craftsmen or, later, factory workers were unusual.

SLAVE LABOUR

The slave trade was commercially very important, too. Huge profits were occasionally made – a fact which partly explains the crammed and pestilential holds of the slaveships in which were confined the human cargoes. They rarely had a death-rate per voyage of less than 10 per cent and sometimes suffered much more appalling mortality. The supposed value of the trade made it a great and contested prize, though the normal return on capital has been much exaggerated. For two centuries it provoked diplomatic wrangling and even war as nation after nation sought to break into it or monopolize it. This testified to the trade's importance in the eyes of statesmen, whether it was economically justified or not.

MECHANICAL ENGINEERING SKILLS IN EUROPE

It was once widely held that the slave trade's profits provided the capital for European industrialization, but this no longer seems plausible. Industrialization was a slow process. Before 1800, though examples of industrial concentration could be found in several European countries, the growth of both manufacturing and extractive industry was still in the main a matter of the multiplication of small-scale artisan production and its technical elaboration, rather than of radically new methods and institutions. Europe had by 1500 an enormous pool of wealth to draw on in her large numbers of skilled craftsmen, already used to investigating new process and exploring new techniques. Two centuries of gunnery had brought mining and metallurgy to a high pitch. Scientific instruments and mechanical clocks testified to a wide diffusion of skill in the making of precision goods. Such advantages as these shaped the early pattern of the industrial age and soon began to reverse a traditional relationship with Asia. For centuries oriental craftsmen had astounded Europeans by their skill and the quality of their work. Asian textiles and ceramics had a superiority which lives in our everyday language: china, muslin, calico, shantung are still familiar words. Then, in the fourteenth and fifteenth centuries, supremacy in some forms of craftsmanship had passed to Europe, notably in mechanical and engineering skills. Asian potentates began to seek Europeans who could teach them how to make effective firearms; they even collected mechanical toys which were the commonplaces of European fairs. Such a reversal of roles was based on Europe's accumulation of skills in traditional occupations and their extension into new fields. This happened usually in towns; craftsmen often travelled from one to another, following demand. So much it is easy to see. What is harder is to see what it was in the European mind which pressed the European craftsman forward and also stimulated the interest of his social betters so that a craze for mechanical engineering is as important an aspect of the age of the Renaissance as is the work of its architects and goldsmiths. After all, this did not happen elsewhere.

INDUSTRIAL GROWTH

EARLY INDUSTRIAL AREAS grew by accretion, often around the centres of established European industries (such as textiles or brewing) closely related to agriculture. This long continued to be true. These old trades had created concentrations of supporting industry. Antwerp had been the great port of entry to Europe for English cloth; as a result, finishing and dyeing establishments appeared there to work up further the commodities flowing through the port. In the English countryside, wool merchants shaped the early pattern of industrial growth by putting out to peasant spinners and weavers the raw materials they needed. The presence of minerals was another locating factor; mining and metallurgy were the most important industrial activities independent of agriculture. But industries could stagnate or even, sometimes, collapse. This seems to have happened to Italy. Its medieval industrial pre-eminence disappeared in the sixteenth century while that of the Flemish Low Countries and western and southern Germany – the old Carolingian heartland –

Carved by a Danish woodworker c.1600, this bas-relief shows skilled clockmakers building a mechanical clock.

Dating from 1801, this painting portrays the English Coalbrookdale iron-smelting works by night. The works was founded by the pioneering iron master Abraham Darby (c.1678–1717), who was the first person successfully to use coke to smelt iron. His grandson, also called Abraham Darby (1750–1791), designed and produced the world's first cast-iron bridge, at the Coalbrookdale foundry in 1779.

lasted another century or so until it began to be clear that England, the Dutch Netherlands and Sweden were the new industrial leaders. In the eighteenth century Russia's extractive industries would add her to this list. By that time, too, other factors were beginning to enter the equation of economic development as organized science was being brought to bear on industrial techniques and state policy shaped industry both consciously and unconsciously.

INFLATION

The long-term picture of overall expansion and growth obviously requires much qualification. Dramatic fluctuations could easily occur even in the nineteenth century, when a bad harvest could lead to runs on banks and a contraction of demand for manufactured goods big enough to be called a slump. This reflected the growing development and integration of the economy. It could cause new forms of distress. Not long after 1500, for example, it began to be noticed that prices were rising with unprecedented speed. Locally this trend was sometimes very sharp indeed, doubling costs in a year. Though nothing like this rate was anywhere maintained for long the general effect seems to have been a roughly fourfold rise in European prices in a century. Given modern rates of inflation, this does not seem very shocking, but it was quite novel and bound to have great and grave repercussions. Among those who owned some property, some benefited and some suffered. Some landowners reacted by putting up rents and increasing as much as possible the yields from their feudal dues. Some had to sell out. In this sense, inflation made for social mobility, as it often does. Among the poor, the effects were usually harsh, for the price of agricultural produce shot up and money wages did not keep pace. Real wages therefore fell. This was sometimes made worse by local factors, too. In England, for example, high wool prices tempted landlords to enclose common land and thus remove it from common use in order to put sheep on it. The wretched peasant grazier starved and, thus, as one famous contemporary comment put it, "sheep ate men". Everywhere in the central third of the century there were popular revolts and a running disorder which reveal both the incomprehensibility and the severity of what was going on. Everywhere it was the extremes of society which felt the pinch of inflation most sharply; to the poor it brought starvation while kings were pinched because they had to spend more than anyone else.

Much ink has been spent by historians on explaining this century-long price rise. They no longer feel satisfied with the explanation first put forward by contemporary observers, that the essential cause was a new supply of bullion which followed the opening of the New World mines by the Spanish; inflation was well under way before American bullion began to arrive in any significant quantity, even if gold later aggravated things. Probably the fundamental pressure always came from a population whose numbers were increasing when big advances in productivity still lay in the future. The rise in prices continued until the beginning of the seventeenth century. Then it began occasionally even to show signs of falling until a slower increase was resumed around 1700.

A NEW SOCIAL ORDER

THE TWENTIETH CENTURY needs no reminders that social change can quickly follow economic change. We have little belief in the immutability of social forms and institutions. Three hundred years ago, many men and women believed them to be virtually God-given and the result was that although social changes took place in the aftermath of

By the Flemish painter David Teniers the Younger (1610–1690), this portrayal of *Peasants in the Tavern* dates from the second half of the 17th century. Not everyone had equal access to the foodstuffs that became increasingly available as international trade grew. The peasant's diet was limited, monotonous and generally lacking in meat. However, the consumption of wine, beer, cider and liquor became a common way of filling empty hours and stomachs.

Painted by Caravaggio (1571–1610), *The Fortune-Teller* dates from c.1594. Despite people's greater knowledge of the world, the cultivation of reason and the advance of science, strong superstitious beliefs remained common in 16th-century Europe.

inflation (and, it must be said, for many other reasons) they were muffled and masked by the persistence of old forms. Superficially and nominally much of European society remained unchanged between 1500 and 1800 or thereabouts. Yet the economic realities underlying it changed a great deal. Appearances were deceptive.

Rural life had already begun to show this in some countries before 1500. As agriculture became more and more a matter of business (though by no means only because of that), traditional rural society had to change. Forms were usually preserved, and the results were more and more incongruous. Although feudal lordship still existed in France in the 1780s it was by then less a social reality than an economic device. The "seigneur" might never see his tenants, might not be of noble blood, and might draw nothing from his lordship except sums of money which represented his claims on his tenants' labour, time and produce.

Further east, the feudal relationship remained more of a reality. This in part reflected an alliance of rulers and nobles to take advantage of the new market for grain and timber in the growing population of western and southern Europe. They tied peasants to the land and exacted heavier and heavier labour services. In Russia serfdom became the very basis of society.

THE ENGLISH NOBILITY

In England even the commercialized "feudalism" which existed in France had gone long before 1800, and noble status conferred no legal privilege beyond the rights to be summoned to a parliament (their other legal distinction was that like most of the other subjects of King George III, they could not vote in the election of a Member of Parliament). The English nobility was a tiny set; until the end of the eighteenth century the House of Lords had fewer than two hundred hereditary members, whose status could only be transmitted to their one direct heir. Consequently, there did not exist in England the large class of noble men and women, all enjoying extensive legal privileges separating them from the rest of the population, such as there was almost universally elsewhere in Europe. In France there were perhaps a quarter of a million nobles on the eve of the Revolution. All had important legal and formal rights; the corresponding legal order in England could comfortably have been assembled in the hall of an Oxford college and would have had rights correspondingly less impressive.

On the other hand, the wealth and social influence of English landowners was immense. Below the peerage stretched the ill-defined class of English gentlemen, linked at the top to the peers' families and disappearing at the other end into the ranks of prosperous farmers and merchants who were eminently respectable but not "gentlefolk". Its permeability was of enormous value in promoting cohesion and mobility. Gentlemanly status could be approached by enrichment, by professional distinction, or by personal merit. It was essentially a matter of a shared code of behaviour, still reflecting the aristocratic concept of honour, but one civilized by the purging away of its exclusiveness, its gothicisms and its legal supports. In the seventeenth and eighteenth centuries the idea of the gentleman became one of the formative influences of English history.

CHANGES IN EUROPEAN RULING HIERARCHIES

It is true that ruling hierarchies differed in all countries. Contrasts could be drawn right across Europe. There would be nothing tidy about the result. None the less, a broad tendency towards social change which strained old forms is observable in many countries by 1700. In the most advanced countries it brought new ideas about what constituted status and how it should be recognized. Though not complete, there was a shift from personal ties to market relationships as a

This 16th-century engraving shows Queen Elizabeth I of England presiding over a meeting of Parliament. The commoners were already beginning to challenge policies laid down by the Crown and its noble councillors.

way of defining people's rights and expectations, and a shift from a corporate vision of society to an individualist one. This was most notable in the United Provinces, the republic which emerged in the Dutch Netherlands during this era. It was in effect ruled by merchants, particularly those of Amsterdam, the centre of Holland, its richest province. Here the landed nobility had never counted for as much as the mercantile and urban oligarchs.

RESPECT FOR ARISTOCRATS

Nowhere else in Europe had social change gone as far by 1789 as in Great Britain and the United Provinces. Elsewhere questioning of traditional status had barely begun. Figaro, the valet-hero of a notably successful eighteenth-century French comedy, jibed that his aristocratic master had done nothing to deserve his privileges beyond giving himself the trouble to be born. This was recognized at the time as a dangerous and subversive idea, but it need not have caused much alarm. Europe was still soaked in the assumptions of aristocracy (and was to be for a long time, even after 1800). Degrees of exclusiveness varied, but the distinction between noble and non-noble remained crucial. Though alarmed aristocrats accused them of doing so, kings

would nowhere ally with commoners against them even in the last resort. Kings were aristocrats, too; it was their trade, one of them said. Only the coming of a great revolution in France changed things much and then hardly at all outside that country before the end of the century. As the nineteenth century began, it looked as if most Europeans still respected noble blood. All that had changed was that not quite so many people still automatically thought it was a distinction which ought to be reflected in laws.

Just as people began to feel that to describe society in terms of orders with legally distinct rights and obligations no longer expressed its reality, so also they ceased to feel so sure that religion upheld a particular social hierarchy. It was still for a long time possible to believe that:

The rich man in his castle,
the poor man at his gate,
God made them, high and lowly,
and ordered their estate

as an Ulsterwoman put it in the nineteenth century, but this was not quite the same thing as saying that a fixed unchanging order was the expression of God's will. Even by 1800 a few people were beginning to think God rather liked the rich man to show the wisdom of God's way by having made his

own way in the world rather than by inheriting his father's place. "Government is a contrivance of human wisdom for the satisfaction of human wants," said an eighteenth-century Irishman, and he was a conservative, too. A broad utilitarianism was coming to be the way more and more people assessed institutions in advanced countries, social institutions among them.

STRAINS

The old formal hierarchies were under most pressure where strain was imposed upon them by increasing economic mobility, by the growth of towns, by the rise of a market economy, by the appearance of new commercial opportunities and by the spread of literacy and awareness. Broadly speaking, three situations can be distinguished. In the East, in Russia, and almost to the same extent in Poland or east Prussia and Hungary, agrarian society was still so little disturbed by new developments that the traditional social pattern was not only intact but all but unchallenged at the end of the eighteenth century. In these landlocked countries, safe from the threats to the existing order implicit in the commercial development of maritime Europe, the traditional ruling classes usually not only retained their position but had often showed that they could actually enlarge their privileges. In a second group of countries, there was enough of a clash between the economic and social worlds which were coming into being and the existing order to provoke demands for change. When political

The 16th century was a desperate time for France. The government went bankrupt, inflation soared and the country was plagued by the terror and cruelty of a religious civil war. However, the French court maintained its lavish rituals, as shown by this painting, which dates from 1581 and depicts a dance at the court of King Henry III.

London's role as a centre for national and international commerce brought the city considerable wealth. This painting by the English artist William Marlow (1740–1813) shows a busy wharf close to London Bridge.

circumstances permitted its resolution, these would demand satisfaction, though they could be contained for a time. France was the outstanding example, but in some of the German states, Belgium and parts of Italy there were signs of the same sort of strain. The third group of countries were those relatively open societies, such as England, the Netherlands and, across the sea, British North America, where the formal distinctions of society already meant less by comparison with wealth (or even talent), legal rights were widely diffused, economic opportunity was felt to be widespread, and wage-dependency was very marked. Even in the sixteenth century, English society seems much more fluid than that of continental countries and, indeed, when the North Americans came to give themselves a new constitution in the

eighteenth century they forbade the conferring of hereditary titles. In these countries individualism had a scope almost untrammelled by law, whatever the real restraints of custom and opportunity.

THE "ADVANCED" EUROPEAN COUNTRIES

It is only too easy in a general account such as this, though, to be over-precise, over-definite. Even the suggested rough tripartite division blurs too much. There were startling contrasts within societies we must misinterpret if we think of them as homogeneous. In the advanced countries there was still much that we should find strange, even antediluvian. The towns of England, France and Germany were for the most part wrapped in a comfortable provincialism lorded over by narrow merchant oligarchies, successful guildsmen or cathedral chapters. Yet Chartres, contentedly rooted in its medieval countryside and medieval ways, its eighteenth-century population still the same size as five hundred years earlier, was part of the same country as Nantes or Bordeaux, thriving, bustling ports which were only two of several making up the dynamic sector of the French economy. Even the nineteenth century would find its immediate forebears unprogressive; far be it from us, therefore, to predicate the existence of a mature and clearly defined individualist and capitalist society wholly conscious of itself as such in any European country. What marked the countries we might call "advanced" was a tendency to move further and faster in that direction than the great majority of the rest of the world.

Sometimes this won them admiration by would-be reformers. One great questioner of the status quo, Voltaire, was greatly struck by the fact that even in the early eighteenth century a great merchant could be as esteemed and respected in England as was a nobleman. He may have slightly exaggerated and he certainly blurred some important nuances, yet it is remarkable – and a part of the story of the rise of Great Britain to world power – that the political class which governed eighteenth-century England was a landed class and fiercely reflected landed values, yet constantly took care to defend the commercial interests of the country and accepted the leadership and guidance in this of the collective wisdom of the City of London. Though people went on talking of a political division between the "moneyed" and the "landed" interest, and though politics long remained a matter of disputed places and conflicting traditions within the landed class, interests which in other countries

would have conflicted with these nevertheless prospered and were not alienated. The explanations must be complex. Some, like the commercialization of British agriculture, go far back into the history of the previous century; some, such as the growth of facilities for private investment in the government and commercial world, were much more recent.

THE DOMINANT NORTHWESTERN STATES

The coincidence of the advanced social evolution of the Netherlands and Great Britain with their economic, and especially their commercial, success is striking. This was once largely attributed to their religion: as a result of a great upheaval within Christendom both had ceased to be dominated by the Catholic Church. Anti-clericals in the eighteenth century and sociologists in the twentieth sought to explore and exploit this coincidence; Protestantism, it was said, provided an ethic

The busy market and washing place of Antwerp, Flanders, were painted by Joost de Momper in 1443. The success of the annual regional and national festivals that were held in Antwerp had attracted new wealth and inhabitants to the growing city.

for capitalism. This no longer seems plausible. There were too may Catholic capitalists, for one thing, and they were often successful. France and Spain were still important trading countries in the eighteenth century and the first seems to have enjoyed for much of it something like the same rates of growth as great Britain, though she was later to fall behind. They were both countries with Atlantic access, and it was those which had tended to show economic growth ever since the sixteenth century. Yet this is not an explanation which goes very far, either. Scotland – northern, Protestant and Atlantic – long remained backward, poor and feudal. There was more to the differences separating Mediterranean and eastern Europe from the north and west than simple geographical position and more than one factor to the explanation of differing rates of modernization. The progress of English and Dutch agriculture, for example, probably owes more to the relative scarcity of land in each country than to anything else.

This painting by Jan Vermeer of Delft (1632–1675), entitled *The Visit*, depicts two members of the settled and orderly middle class that was characteristic of the Netherlands by the 17th century. Most Dutch people from this social background appreciated fine fabrics, works of art and elegant pieces of furniture, while retaining their sense of the spiritual value of austerity.

THE EUROPEAN EAST

The European East remained backward. The social and economic structure remained fundamentally unchanged until the nineteenth century. Deep-rooted explanations have been offered – that, for example, a shorter growing season and less rich soils than were to be found further west gave it from the start a poorer return on seed, and therefore handicapped it economically in the crucial early stages of agricultural growth. It had man-made handicaps, too. Settlement there had long been open to disturbance by Central Asian nomads, while on its southern flank lay the Balkans and the frontier with Turkey, for many centuries a zone of warfare, raiding and banditry. In some areas (Hungary for example) the effects of Turkish rule had been so bad as to depopulate the country. When it was reacquired for Europe, care was taken to tie the peasantry to the land. In the Russia which emerged from Muscovy in this period, too, the serf population grew larger as a proportion of the whole. Harsher law guaranteed their masters control of the peasants. In other eastern countries (Prussia was one), the powers of landlords over tenants were strengthened. This was more than just a kingly indulgence of aristocracies which might, if not placated, turn against royal authority. It was also a device for economic development. Not for the first time, nor the last, economic progress went with social injustice; serfdom was a way of making available one of the resources needed if land was to be made productive, just as forced labour was in many other countries at many other times.

One result which is still in some degree visible was a Europe divided roughly along the Elbe. To the west lay countries evolving slowly by 1800 towards more open social forms. To the east lay authoritarian govern-

A NEW KIND OF SOCIETY: EARLY MODERN EUROPE

35

A reading from a tragedy by the celebrated writer Voltaire is given in Madame Geoffrin's drawing-room, or *salon*, in 1775. French noblewomen and ladies of the upper bourgeoisie organized conferences, concerts and scientific experiments, which, in some cases, converted their drawing-rooms into distinguished academies.

ments presiding over agrarian societies where a minority of landholders enjoyed great powers over a largely tied peasantry. In this area towns did not often prosper as they had done for centuries in the West. They tended to be overtaxed islands in a rural sea, unable to attract from the countryside the labour they needed because of the extent of serfdom. Over great tracts of Poland and Russia even a money economy barely existed. Much of later European history was implicit in this difference between east and west.

WOMEN IN EUROPE

The east–west divide was discernible in informal institutions, too, in the way, for example, in which women were treated, though here another division could be drawn, that between Mediterranean Europe and the north, which was in due course extended to run between Latin and North America. Formally and legally, little changed anywhere

in these centuries; the legal status of women remained what it had been and this was only to be questioned right at the end of this period. Nevertheless, the real independence of women and, in particular, of upper-class women, does seem to have been enlarged in the more advanced countries. Even in the fifteenth century it had been remarked by foreigners that Englishwomen enjoyed unusual freedom. This lead does not seem to have diminished, but in the eighteenth century there are signs that in France, at least, a well-born woman could enjoy considerable real independence.

This was in part because the eighteenth century brought the appearance of a new sort of upper-class life, one which had room for other social gatherings than those of a royal court, and one increasingly independent of religious and family ritual. At the end of the seventeenth century we hear of men in London meeting in the coffee-houses from which the first clubs were to spring. Soon there appears the *salon*, the social gathering of friends and acquaintances in a lady's drawing-room which was especially the creation of the French; some eighteenth-century *salons* were important intellectual centres and show that it had become proper and even fashionable for a woman to show an interest in things of the mind other than religion. On one of the occasions on which Madame de Pompadour, the mistress of Louis XV, was painted, she chose to have included in the picture a book – Montesquieu's socio-logical treatise, *De l'esprit des lois*. But even when women did not aspire to blue stock-ings, the *salon* and the appearance of a society independent of the court presented them with a real, if limited, escape from the confinement of the family, which, together with religious and professional gatherings, had until then been virtually the only struc-tures within which even men might seek social variety and diversion.

THE UNQUESTIONED CERTAINTIES OF EUROPEAN SOCIETY

By the end of the eighteenth century we have arrived at the age of the female artist and novelist and of acceptance of the fact that spinsterhood need not mean retirement to a cloister. Where such changes came from is not easy to see. In the early years of the century the *Spectator* already thought it worth while to address itself to women readers as well as men, which suggests that we should look a fair way back. Perhaps it helped that the eighteenth century produced such conspicu-ous examples of women of great political influence – an English queen and four empresses (one Austrian and three Russian) all ruled in their own right, often with success. But it is not possible to say so with confidence for the prehistory of female emancipation still largely awaits study.

Finally, none of this touched the life of the overwhelming majority in even the most advanced societies of early modern Europe. There had not yet come into being the mass industrial jobs which would provide the first great force to prize apart the unquestioned certainties of traditional life for most men and women alike. Though they may have weighed most heavily in the primitive villages of Poland or in a southern Spain where Moorish influences had intensified the subordination and seclusion of women, those certainties were everywhere still heavy in 1800.

Madame de Pompadour (1721–1764) is depicted in this portrait by the celebrated French painter François Boucher (1703–1770). The influential mistress of Louis XV, Madame de Pompadour befriended Boucher and played an important role in his career, commissioning countless paintings from him. In return, he painted her portrait on numerous occasions.

2 AUTHORITY AND ITS CHALLENGERS

IN 1800 MANY EUROPEANS still held ideas about social and political organization which would have been comprehensible and appropriate four hundred years earlier. The "Middle Ages" no more came to a sudden end in this respect than in many others. Ideas about society and government which may reasonably be described as "medieval" survived as effective forces over a wide area and during the centuries more and more social facts had been fitted into them. Broadly speaking, what has been called the "corporate" organization of society, the grouping of men in bodies with legal privileges which protected their members and defined their status was still the rule in the eighteenth century in continental Europe. Over much of its central and eastern zones, as we have noted, serfdom had grown more rigid and more widespread.

Many continuities in political institutions were obvious. The Holy Roman Empire still existed in 1800 as it had done in 1500; so did the temporal power of the pope. A descendant of the Capetians was still king of France (though he no longer came from the same branch of the family as in 1500 and, indeed, was in exile). Even in England and as late as 1820, a king's champion rode in full armour into Westminster Hall at the coronation banquet of King George IV, to uphold that monarch's title against all comers. In most countries it was still taken for granted that the state was a confessional entity, that religion and society were intertwined and that the authority of the Church was established by law. Although such ideas had been much challenged and in some countries had undergone grievous reverses, in this as in many

In this 15th-century Italian picture of a battle, the prince is still represented as the leader of his men as his troops come face to face with soldiers from another faction. From this period onward, however, it became increasingly common for kings and princes to employ generals to lead their armies.

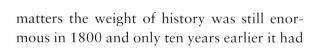

Machiavelli on the use of power

"From this arises the following question: whether it is better to be loved than feared, or the reverse. The answer is that one would like to be both the one and the other; but because it is difficult to combine them, it is far better to be feared than loved if you cannot be both. ... Men worry less about doing an injury to one who makes himself loved than to one who makes himself feared. The bond of love is one which men, wretched creatures that they are, break when it is to their advantage to do so; but fear is strengthened by a dread of punishment which is always effective.

"The prince must none the less make himself feared in such a way that, if he is not loved, at least he escapes being hated. For fear is quite compatible with an absence of hatred; and the prince can always avoid hatred if he abstains from the property of his subjects and citizens and from their women. If, even so, it proves necessary to execute someone, this is to be done only when there is proper justification and manifest reason for it. But above all a prince must abstain from the property of others; because men sooner forget the death of their father than the loss of their patrimony."

An extract from *The Prince* by Niccolò Machiavelli (1469–1527), translated by George Bull.

matters the weight of history was still enormous in 1800 and only ten years earlier it had been even heavier.

STATE AUTHORITY

When all the continuity in European history is acknowledged, it was nevertheless the general tendency of the three centuries between 1500 and 1800 to dissolve or at least weaken old social and political bonds characteristic of medieval government. Power and authority had instead tended to flow towards the central concentration provided by the state, and away from "feudal" arrangements of personal dependence. (The very invention of the "feudal" idea as a technical term of law was in fact the work of the seventeenth century and it suggests the age's need to define something whose reality was ebbing away.) The idea of Christendom, too, though still important in emotional, even subconscious ways, effectively lost any political reality in this period. Papal authority had begun to suffer at the hands of national sentiment in the age of the Schism and that of the Holy Roman emperors had been of small account since the fourteenth century. Nor did any new unifying principle emerge to integrate Europe. The test case was the Ottoman threat. Christian princes exposed to the Muslim

The Italian statesman and writer Niccolò Machiavelli, one-time adviser to the powerful Medici rulers of Florence, is considered by many as the originator of a pragmatic and ruthless political ethos in which the end justifies the means.

onslaught might appeal to their fellow-Christians for help, popes might still use the rhetoric of crusade, but the reality, as the Turks well knew, was that Christian states would follow their own interest and ally with the infidel, if necessary. This was the era of *Realpolitik*, of the conscious subordination of principle and honour to intelligent calculation of the interests of the state. It is curious that in an age in which Europeans more and more agreed that greater distinctions of culture separated them (to their credit, they were sure) from other civilizations they paid little attention to institutions (and did nothing to create

new ones) which acknowledged their essential unity. Only the occasional philosopher advocated the building of something which transcended the state. Perhaps, though, it is just in a new awareness of cultural superiority that the explanation lies. Europe was entering an age of triumphant expansion and did not need shared institutions to tell her so. Indeed, the authority of states, and so the power of their governments, waxed in these centuries.

Here it is important not to be misled by forms. For all the arguments about who should exercise it and a mass of political writing which suggested all sorts of limits on it, the general trend was towards acceptance of the idea of legislative sovereignty – that is, Europeans came to feel that, provided the authority of the state were in the right hands, there should be no restriction upon its power to make laws.

QUESTIONING THE EXISTENCE OF FUNDAMENTAL LAWS

This was an enormous break with the thinking of the past. To a medieval European the idea that there might not be rights and rules above interference by any individual, legal immunities and chartered freedoms inaccessible to change by subsequent lawmakers, fundamental laws which would always be respected, or laws of God which could never be contravened by those of human beings, would have been social and juridical, as well as theological, blasphemy. English lawyers of the seventeenth century floundered about in disagreement over what the fundamental laws of the land might be, but all thought some must exist. A century later the leading legal minds of France were doing just the same. In the end, nevertheless, there emerged in both countries (as, to a greater or lesser degree, in most others) the acceptance of the idea that a

European officials who drew up and authenticated public or private documents required a good legal and cultural education. A room in the College of Public Notaries is depicted in this 16th-century French manuscript.

sovereign, legally unrestrained lawmaking power was the characteristic mark of the state. Yet this took a long time. For most of the history of early modern Europe the emergence of the modern sovereign state was obscured by the fact that the most widely prevalent form of government was monarchy. Struggles about the powers of rulers make up much of European history in these centuries and sometimes it is hard to see exactly what is at stake. The claims of kings and queens, after all, could be challenged on two quite distinct grounds: there was resistance based on the principle that it would be wrong for any government to have powers such as some monarchs claimed (and this might be termed the medieval or conservative defence of freedom) and there was resistance based on the principle that such powers could properly exist, but were being gathered into the wrong hands (and this can be called the modern or liberal defence of freedom). In practice, the two claims are often inextricably confused, but the confusion is itself a significant indicator of changing ideas.

THE RISE OF ABSOLUTE MONARCHY

Once away from legal principle, the strengthening of the state showed itself in the growing ability of royal rulers to get their way. One indicator was the nearly universal decline in the sixteenth and seventeenth centuries of the representative institutions which had appeared in many countries in the later Middle Ages. By 1789, most of Western (if not Central and Eastern) Europe was ruled by monarchs little hindered by representative bodies; the main exception was in Great Britain. Monarchs began in the sixteenth century to enjoy powers which would have seemed remarkable to medieval barons and burghers. The phenomenon is sometimes described as the rise of absolute monarchy. If we do not exaggerate a monarch's chances of actually carrying out his or her declared wishes (for many practical checks might exist to royal power which were just as restricting as medieval immunities or a representative assembly), the term is acceptable. Almost everywhere, the relative strength of rulers *vis-à-vis* their rivals increased greatly from the sixteenth century onwards. New financial resources gave them standing armies and artillery to use against great nobles who could not afford them. Sometimes the monarchy was able to ally itself with the slow growth of a sense of nationhood in imposing order on

King Louis XIV of France (1638–1715), shown here visiting the Académie Royale des Sciences in 1667, saw himself as a role model for Europe's absolute monarchs. "L'état c'est moi," he once declared – "I am the state."

the over-mighty. In many countries the late fifteenth century had brought a new readiness to accept royal government if it would guarantee order and peace. There were special reasons in almost every case, but nearly everywhere monarchs raised themselves further above the level of the greatest nobles and buttressed their new pretensions to respect and authority with cannon and taxation. The obligatory sharing of power with great subjects whose status entitled them de facto and sometimes *de jure* to office, ceased to weigh so heavily upon monarchs. England's Privy Council under the Tudors was a meritocracy as well as a gathering of magnates.

THE "RENAISSANCE STATE"

Changes in the structures of monarchy in Europe during the sixteenth and early seventeenth centuries brought about the appearance of what some have called the "Renaissance State". This is a rather grandiose term for swollen bureaucracies, staffed by royal employees and directed by aspirations to centralization, but clear enough if we remember the implied antithesis: the medieval kingdom, whose governmental functions were often in large measure delegated to feudal and personal dependents or to corporations (of which the Church was the greatest). Of course, neither model of political organization existed historically in a pure form. There had always been royal officials, "new men" of obscure origin, and governments today still delegate tasks to non-governmental bodies. There was no sudden transition to the modern "state": it took centuries and often used old forms. In England, the Tudors seized on the existing institution of royal Justices of the Peace to weld the local squires into the structure of royal government. This was yet another stage in a long process of undermining seigneurial authority which elsewhere still had centuries of life before it. Even in England, too, as Tudor rebellions showed, noblemen had long to be treated with care if they were not to be fatally antagonized. Rebellion was not an exceptional but a continuing fact of life for the sixteenth-century statesman. Royal troops might prevail in the end, but no monarch wanted to be reduced to reliance on force. As a famous motto had it, artillery was the last argument of kings. The history of the French nobility's turbulence right down to the middle of the seventeenth century, of the effects of antagonizing local interest in England during the same period, of Habsburg attempts to unify their territories at the expense of local magnates, all show this. The United Kingdom had its last feudal rebellion in 1745; other countries had theirs still later.

In many European countries the birth of the "Renaissance State" was accompanied by a reorganization of the army, the judiciary and the economy. This 16th-century miniature depicts a session of the Chamber of the Exchequer in Paris, an institution created to oversee the French financial system.

TAXATION

Taxation, too, because of the danger of rebellion and the inadequacy of administrative machinery to collect it, could not be pressed very far, yet officials and armies had to be paid for. One way was to allow officials to charge fees or levy perquisites on those who needed their services. For obvious reasons, this was not a complete answer. The raising of greater sums by the ruler was therefore necessary. Something might still be done

A new body of professional diplomats emerged during the Renaissance. These French ambassadors were painted by Hans Holbein the Younger.

The collection of taxes, the revenue from which had almost always been spent in advance, was usually in the hands of money-lenders or bankers. These, in turn, sent their intermediaries to collect the money. This 16th-century painting of a pair of tax collectors is by Marinus van Reymerswaele.

by exploiting royal domains. But all monarchs, sooner or later, were driven back to seek new taxation and it was a problem few could solve. There were technical problems here which could not be dealt with until the nineteenth century or even later, but for three centuries great fertility of imagination was to be shown in inventing new taxes. Broadly speaking, only consumption (through indirect taxes such as customs and excise or taxes on sale, or through requiring licences and authorizations to trade which had to be paid for) or real property could be tapped by the tax-gatherer. Usually, this bore disproportionately upon the poorest, who spent a larger part of their small disposable income on necessities

than the wealthy. Nor was it easy to stop a landowner from passing his tax burdens along to the man at the bottom of the property pyramid. Taxation, too, was particularly hindered by the surviving medieval idea of legal immunity. In 1500 it was generally accepted that there were areas, persons and spheres of action which were specially protected from invasion by the power of the rule. They might be defended by an irrevocable royal grant in past ages such as were the privileges of many cities, by contractual agreement such as the English Magna Carta was said to be, by immemorial custom, or by divine law. The supreme example was the Church. Its properties were not normally subject to lay taxation, it had jurisdiction in its courts of matters inaccessible to royal justice, and it controlled important social and economic institutions – marriage, for example. But a province, or a profession, or a family might also enjoy immunities, usually from royal jurisdiction or taxation. Nor was royal standing uniform. Even the French king was only a duke in Brittany and that made a difference to what he was entitled to do there. Such facts were the realities which the "Renaissance State" had to live with. It could do no other than accept their survival, even if the future lay with the royal bureaucrats and their files.

HERESY AND HUMANISM

IN THE EARLY SIXTEENTH CENTURY, a great crisis, which shook Western Christianity and destroyed forever the old medieval unity of the faith, much accelerated the consolidation of royal power. The Protestant Reformation began as just one more dispute over religious authority, the calling in question of the papal claims whose formal and theoretical structure had successfully survived

This painting, from the school of Hans Holbein the Younger, depicts Sir Thomas More (1478–1535), the English Roman Catholic humanist, statesman and author of *Utopia* (1516). More sympathized with Erasmus of Rotterdam's proposals for the reform of the Church.

fifteenth century another current in religious life, perhaps more profoundly subversive than heresy, because, unlike heresy, it contained forces which might in the end cut at the roots of the traditional religious outlook itself. This was the learned, humanistic, rational, sceptical intellectual movement which, for want of a better word, we may call Erasmian after the man who embodied its ideals most clearly in the eyes of contemporaries, and who was the first Dutchman to play a leading role in European history. He was profoundly loyal to his faith; he knew himself to be a Christian and that meant, unquestionably, that he remained within the Church. But of that Church he had an ideal which embodied a vision of a possible reformation. He sought a simpler devotion and a purer pastorate.

so many challenges. Thus, in origin at least, it was a thoroughly medieval phenomenon. But important as that was, that was not to be the whole story of the Reformation and far from exhausts its political significance. Given that it also detonated a cultural revolution, there is no reason to question its traditional standing as the start of modern history.

ERASMIAN IDEAS

There was nothing new about demands for reform. The sense that papacy and *curia* did not necessarily serve the interests of all Christians was well grounded by 1500. Some critics had already gone on from this to doctrinal dissent. The deep, uneasy devotional swell of the fifteenth century had expressed a search for new answers to spiritual questions but also a willingness to look for them outside the limits laid down by ecclesiastical authority. Heresy had never been blotted out, it had only been contained. Popular anticlericalism was an old and widespread phenomenon. There had also appeared in the

Erasmus of Rotterdam (1467–1536) is shown at his desk, in a portrait by Hans Holbein the Younger (c.1497–1543).

This portrait of Martin Luther (1483–1546), the German theologian who was the leading figure of the German Reformation, dates from the first half of the 16th century.

Martin Luther's theses

5.　The Pope cannot and does not intend to pardon any sentence either dictated by him or imposed by canonical laws.

21.　Consequently, those who preach of pardons are wrong when they say that through papal pardons man is free of all sentence and is saved.

32.　Those who believe their salvation to be guaranteed through indulgences will be condemned forever with their masters.

82.　For example: Why does the Pope not empty purgatory as an act of holy charity and taking into account the utmost necessity of these souls – the most justified of motives – if with the ill-fated money destined for the construction of the basilica – the most banal motive – he redeems infinite souls?

Extracts from Martin Luther's 95 theses against indulgences ("Disputatio pro declarationes virtutis indulgentiarum"), 1517.

Though he did not challenge the authority of the Church or papacy, in a subtler way he challenged authority in principle, for his scholarly work had implications which were deeply subversive, and so was the tone of the correspondence which he conducted with colleagues the length and breadth of Europe. They learnt from him to disentangle their logic and therefore the teaching of the faith from the scholastic mummifications of Aristotelian philosophy. In his Greek New Testament he made available a firm basis for argument on doctrine at a time when Greek was again becoming widespread. Erasmus, too, was the exposer of the spuriousness of texts on which bizarre dogmatic structures had been raised.

Yet Erasmus and others who shared his viewpoint did not attack religious authority outright or turn ecclesiastical into universal issues. They were good Catholics. Humanism, like heresy, discontent with clerical behaviour and the cupidity of princes, was something in the air at the beginning of the sixteenth century, waiting – as many things had long waited – for the man and the occasion which would make them into a religious revolution. No other term is adequate to describe what followed the unwitting act of a German monk. His name was Martin Luther and in 1517 he launched a movement which was to end by fragmenting a Christian unity intact in the West since the disappearance of the Arians.

MARTIN LUTHER

Unlike Erasmus, the international man, Luther lived all his life except for brief absences in a small German town, Wittenberg, almost at the back of beyond on the Elbe. He was an Augustinian monk, deeply read in theology, somewhat tormented in spirit, who had already come to the conclusion that he must preach the Scriptures in a new light, to present God as a forgiving God, not a punitive one. This need not have made him a revolutionary; the orthodoxy of his views was never in question until he quarrelled with the papacy. He had been to Rome, and he had not liked what he saw there, for the papal city seemed a worldly place and its ecclesiastical rulers no better than they should be. This did not dispose him to feel warmly towards an itinerant Dominican who came to Saxony only as a pedlar of indulgences. These documents were papal certificates that the possessor, in consideration of payment (which went towards the building of the new and magnificent St Peter's then rising in Rome), would be assured that some of the penalties incurred by him for sin would be remitted in the next world. Accounts of the preaching of this man were brought to Luther by peasants who had heard him and bought their indulgences. Research has made it clear that what had been said to them was not only misleading but outrageous; the crudity of the transaction promoted by the preacher displays one of the most unattractive faces of medieval Catholicism. It infuriated Luther, almost obsessed as he was by the overwhelming seriousness of the transformation necessary in a person's life before he or she could be sure of redemption. He formulated his protests against this and certain other papal practices in a set of ninety-five theses setting out his positive views. In the tradition of the scholarly disputation he posted them in Latin on the door of the castle church in Wittenberg on 21 October 1517. He had also sent the theses to the Archbishop of Mainz, primate

of Germany, who passed them to Rome with a request that Luther be forbidden by his order to preach on this theme. By this time the theses had been put into German and the new information technology had transformed the situation; they were printed and circulated everywhere in Germany. So Luther got the debate he sought. Only the protection of Frederick of Saxony, the ruler of Luther's state, who refused to surrender him, kept him out of danger of his life. The delay in scotching the chicken of heresy in the egg was fatal. Luther's order abandoned him, but his university did not. Soon the papacy found itself confronted by a German national movement of grievance against Rome sustained and inflamed by Luther's own sudden discovery that he was a literary genius of astonishing fluency and productivity, the first to exploit the huge possibilities of the printed pamphlet.

THE REFORMATION

WITHIN TWO YEARS, Luther was being called a Hussite. The Reformation had by then become entangled in German politics. Even in the Middle Ages would-be reformers had looked to secular rulers for help. This did not necessarily mean going outside the fold of the faith; the great Spanish churchman Ximenes had sought to bring to bear the authority of the Catholic monarchs on the problems facing the Spanish Church. Monarchs tended not to like heretics; their duty was to uphold the true faith. Nevertheless, an appeal to lay authority could open the way to changes which went further perhaps, than, their authors had intended, and this, it seems, was the case with Luther. His arguments had rapidly carried him beyond the desirability and grounds of reform in practice to the questioning of papal

The evolution of printing

Printing played a prominent role in the expansion of literacy. By the 17th century, books had become commonplace in the homes of wealthy people who had received some education, and the ownership of a private library became a status symbol for the rich and cultured. Most early books were on religious themes: the Reformation and the Counter-Reformation and the controversies that preoccupied Roman Catholics and Protestants at that time acted as a strong stimulus to the production of books. Bibles, prayer books and doctrinal works were, for a long time, the main printed works.

Secular works made ground only gradually. The works of the humanists, with the exception of Erasmus, and the publication of works by classical authors never had more than a limited public. However, published treatises and law compendiums became increasingly common, as the study of law came to be considered an essential part of a gentleman's education. Political works became popular, as did scientific treatises accompanied by illustrations on

metallurgy, mining, machines, mechanical applications, chemistry, agriculture, architecture, urban planning and the building of dykes and canals. Books on the subjects of commercial arithmetic, bookkeeping and other business skills also sold well, although the practical value of such publications was extremely variable.

In the first century of its history, printing was carried out by individuals who combined the roles of typographer, printer, editor and bookseller. They would travel from city to city in search of wealthy patrons and a readership. From the middle of the 16th century, there was a tendency towards a concentration of larger firms and the specialization of functions. Thus, educated scholars composed the page, typesetting became the work of firms with expertise in that process; the owner of a workshop limited himself to administration and proofreading; and the printing was left to skilled, strong men, who, by the beginning of the 18th century, were capable of producing 3,000 pages a day.

This 17th-century woodcut depicts the interior of a printing works in Nuremberg, Germany.

authority and, then, of doctrine. The core of his early protests had not been theological. Nevertheless, he now rejected transubstantiation (replacing it with a view of the eucharist which is even more difficult to grasp) and preached that mortals were justified – that is, set aside for salvation – not by observance of the sacraments only ("works", as this was called), but by faith. This was, clearly, an intensely individualist position. It struck at the root of traditional teaching which saw no salvation possible outside the Church. (Yet, it may be noted, Erasmus, when asked for his view, would not condemn Luther; it was known, moreover, that he thought Luther to have said many valuable things.) In 1520 Luther was excommunicated. Before a wondering audience he burnt the bull of excommunication in the same fire as the books of canon law. He continued to preach

and write. Summoned to explain himself before the imperial Diet, he refused to retract his views. Germany seemed on the verge of civil war. After leaving the Diet under a safe-conduct, he disappeared, kidnapped for his own safety by a sympathetic prince. In 1521 Charles V, the emperor, placed him under the Imperial Ban; Luther was now an outlaw.

Luther's doctrines, which he extended to condemnations of confession and absolution and clerical celibacy, by now appealed to many Germans. His followers spread them by preaching and by distributing his German translation of the New Testament. Lutheranism was also a political fact; the German princes, who entangled it in their own complicated relations with the emperor and his vague authority over them, ensured this. Wars ensued and the word "Protestant" came into use. By 1555, Germany was

This engraving, dating from 1555, depicts the Diet of Augsburg, held on 30 June 1548, during which the German princes met in the presence of the emperor Charles V. The factional fighting between Catholics and Protestants that followed continued until the Peace of Augsburg of 1555.

This portrait depicts Huldreich Zwingli (1484–1531), the priest who introduced the Reformation to Switzerland. The optimism and equality of Zwingli's Christian humanism contrasted with Calvin's beliefs, which were founded in the concept of human beings as sinners facing the omnipotent power of God.

irreparably divided into Catholic and Protestant states. This was recognized in agreement at the Diet of Augsburg that the prevailing religion of each state should be that of its ruler, the first European institutionalizing of religious pluralism. It was a curious concession for an emperor who saw himself as the defender of universal Catholicism. Yet it was necessary if he was to keep the loyalty of Germany's princes. In Catholic and Protestant Germany alike, religion now looked as never before to political authority to uphold it in a world of competing creeds.

CALVINISM

By 1555, other varieties of Protestantism had appeared. Some drew on social unrest. Luther soon had to distinguish his own teaching from the views of peasants who involved his

name to justify rebellion against their masters. One radical group were the Anabaptists, persecuted by Catholic and Protestant rulers alike. At Münster in 1534 their leaders' introduction of communism of property and polygamy confirmed their opponents' fears and brought a ferocious suppression upon them. Of other forms of Protestantism, only one demands notice in so general an account as this. Calvinism was to be Switzerland's most important contribution to the Reformation, but it was the creation of a Frenchman, John Calvin. He was a theologian who formulated his essential doctrines while still a young man: the absolute depravity of man after the Fall of Adam and the impossibility of salvation except for those few, the Elect, predestined by God to salvation. If Luther, the Augustinian monk, spoke with the voice of Paul, Calvin evoked the tones of Augustine. It is not easy to understand the attractiveness of this gloomy creed. But to its efficacy, the history not only of

John Calvin the Younger (1509–1564), like other religious leaders, was convinced of the veracity of his own beliefs and the falsity of those of his opponents.

drowned, men beheaded (an apparent reversal of the normal penal practice of a male-dominated European society where women, considered weaker vessels morally and intellectually, were usually indulged with milder punishments than men). The most severe punishments, though, were reserved for those guilty of heresy.

From Geneva, where its pastors were trained, the new sect took root in France, where it won converts among the nobility and had more than 2,000 congregations by 1561. In the Netherlands, England and Scotland and, in the end, Germany, it challenged Lutheranism. It spread also to Poland, Bohemia and Hungary. Thus in its first century it showed a remarkable vigour, surpassing that of Lutheranism which, except in Scandinavia, was never strongly entrenched beyond the German lands which first adopted it.

THE CONSEQUENCES OF THE REFORMATION

The Protestant Reformation still defies summary and simplification. Complex and deep-rooted in its origins, it also owed much to circumstance and was very rich and far-reaching in its effects. In Europe and the Americas it created new ecclesiastical cultures founded on the study of the Bible and preaching, to which it gave an importance sometimes surpassing that of the sacraments. It was to shape the lives of millions by accustoming them to a new and an intense scrutiny of private conduct and conscience (thus, ironically, achieving something long sought by

Geneva, but of France, England, Scotland, the Dutch Netherlands, and British North America all witnessed. The crucial step was conviction of membership of the Elect. As the signs of this were outward adherence to the commandments of God and participation in the sacraments, it was less difficult to achieve such conviction than might be imagined.

Under Calvin, Geneva was not a place for the easy-going. He had drawn up the constitution of a theocratic state which provided the framework for a remarkable exercise in self-government. Blasphemy and witchcraft were punished by death, but this would not have struck contemporaries as surprising. Adultery, too, was a crime in most European countries and one punished by ecclesiastical courts. But Calvin's Geneva took this offence much more seriously and imposed the death penalty for that, too. Adulterous women were

Henry VIII of England (1491–1547), here depicted in a portrait by Hans Holbein the Younger, renounced his subordination to the Catholic Church of Rome in order to establish his leadership of the Church of England, over which he was to have complete control. Although the Protestant reformers paved the way for other European sovereigns to make similar breaks with Rome, it seems likely that the medieval unity of the Church was already doomed, even before the Reformation.

ANNO · ÆTATIS · · SVÆ · XLIX ·

Roman Catholics) and re-created the non-celibate clergy. Negatively, it slighted or at least called in question all existing ecclesiastical institutions and created new political forces in the form of churches which princes could now manipulate for their own ends – often against popes whom they saw simply as princes like themselves.

THE CHURCH OF ENGLAND

CURIOUSLY, NEITHER LUTHERANISM nor Calvinism provoked the first rejection of papal authority by a nation-state. In England a unique religious change arose almost by accident. A new dynasty originating in Wales, the Tudors, had established itself at the end of

POLITICS AND THE CHURCH IN ENGLAND AND EUROPE

Churchmen sympathetic to new doctrines sought to move the Church in England significantly towards continental Protestant ideas in the next reign. Popular reactions were mixed. Some saw this as the satisfaction of old national traditions of dissent from Rome; some resented innovations. From a confused debate and murky politics emerged one literary masterpiece, the Book of Common Prayer, and some martyrs both Catholic and Protestant. The latter were the first to suffer, for there was a reversion to papal authority (and the burning of Protestant heretics) under

the fifteenth century and the second king of this line, Henry VIII, became entangled with the papacy over his wish to dissolve the first of his six marriages in order to remarry and get an heir, an understandable preoccupation. This led to a quarrel and one of the most remarkable assertions of lay authority in the whole sixteenth century; it was also one fraught with significance for England's future. With the support of his parliament, which obediently passed the required legislation, Henry VIII proclaimed himself Head of the Church in England. Doctrinally, he conceived no break with the past; he was, after all, entitled Defender of the Faith by the pope because of a refutation of Luther from the royal pen (his descendant still bears his title). But the assertion of the Royal Supremacy opened the way to an English Church separate from Rome. A vested interest in it was soon provided by a dissolution of monasteries and some other ecclesiastical foundations and the sale of property to their buyers among the aristocracy and gentry.

Mary I (Mary Tudor), Queen of England from 1553 to 1558, was the daughter of Catherine of Aragon and Henry VIII and the wife of Philip II of Spain. She attempted to re-convert her English subjects to Roman Catholicism, unleashing, perhaps unwittingly, a terrible campaign of persecution against Protestants. Mary's early death may have saved her country from civil war.

the fourth Tudor, the unfairly named and unhappy Bloody Mary, perhaps England's most tragic queen. By this time, moreover, the question of religion was thoroughly entangled with national interest and foreign policy, for the states of Europe drew apart more and more on religious grounds.

THE REFORMATION AND THE ENGLISH PARLIAMENT

The English Reformation, which, like the German, was a landmark in the evolution of a national consciousness, was also notable for other reasons. It had been carried out by Act of Parliament and a constitutional question was implicit in the religious settlement: were there any limits to legislative authority? With the accession of Mary's half-sister, Elizabeth I, the pendulum swung back, though for a long time it was unclear how far. Yet Elizabeth insisted, and had Parliament legislate, that she retain the essentials of her father's position; the English Church, or Church of England, as it may henceforth be called, claimed to be Catholic in doctrine but rested on the Royal Supremacy. More important still, because that Supremacy was recognized by Act of

This 16th-century painting represents the St Bartholomew's Day Massacre, which took place in Paris during the night of 23–24 August, 1572. The horror that ensued, as Catholics murdered Protestant Huguenots, made many people question the value of beliefs that could lead to such a blood-bath.

Parliament, England was soon to be at war with a Catholic king of Spain who was well known for his determination to root out heresy in the lands he subjugated. So another national cause was identified with that of Protestantism.

Reformation helped the English parliament to survive when other medieval representative bodies were going under before the new power of monarchs, though this was far from the whole story. A kingdom united since Anglo-Saxon times without provincial assemblies or "estates" which might rival it made it much easier for Parliament to focus national politics than any similar body elsewhere. A royal mistake helped, too; Henry VIII had squandered a great opportunity to achieve a sound basis for absolute monarchy when he rapidly liquidated the mass of property – about a fifth of the land of the whole kingdom – which he held briefly as a result of the dissolutions. Nevertheless, all such imponderables duly weighed, the fact that Henry chose to seek endorsement of his will from the national representative body in creating a national church still seems one of the most crucial decisions in Parliament's history.

THE FRENCH WARS OF RELIGION

Catholic martyrs died under Elizabeth because they were judged traitors, not because they were heretics – but England was far less divided by religion than Germany and France. Sixteenth-century France was tormented and torn by Catholic and Calvinist interests. Each was in essence a group of noble clans, who fought for power in the Wars of Religion, of which nine have been distinguished between 1562 and 1598. At times their struggles brought the French monarchy very low; the nobility of France came near to winning the battle against the centralizing state. Yet, in the end, their divisions benefited a Crown which could use one faction against another. The wretched population of France had to bear the brunt of disorder and devastation until there came to the throne in 1589 (after the murder of his predecessor) a member of a junior branch of the royal family, Henry, king of the little state of Navarre, who became Henry IV of France and inaugurated the Bourbon line whose descendants still claim the French throne. He had been a Protestant, but accepted Catholicism as the condition of his succession, recognizing that Catholicism was the religion most French people would cling to. The Protestants were assured special guarantees which left them a state within a state, the possessors of fortified towns where the king's writ did not run; this very old-fashioned sort of solution assured protection for their religion by creating new immunities. Henry and his successors could then turn to the business of re-establishing the authority of a throne badly shaken by assassination and intrigue. But the French nobility were still far from tamed.

THE COUNTER-REFORMATION

LONG BEFORE THE REIGN of Henry IV of France, religious struggles had been further inflamed by the wave of internal reassessment and innovation within the Roman Church which is called the Counter-Reformation. Its formal expression was a general council, the Council of Trent, summoned in 1545 and meeting in three sessions over the next eighteen years. Bishops from Italy and Spain dominated it. This mattered, for the Reformers challenged Catholicism little in Italy and not at all in Spain. The

Reformation and Counter-Reformation Europe

In the second half of the 16th century, the time of religious reconciliation came to an end. Old conflicts re-emerged and new conflicts began to appear, in the form of confessional confrontations between Reformed and Catholic forces. Political divisions within individual countries began to polarize depending on the different factions' religious leanings: these divisions crossed class barriers and affected every level of society. Thus, political struggles tended to become civil wars and civil wars invited foreign intervention. The year 1562, which marked the outbreak of the Wars of Religion in France, saw the beginning of what some contemporaries called "the century of iron". The map shows the predominantly Protestant and Roman Catholic regions of Europe in about 1600.

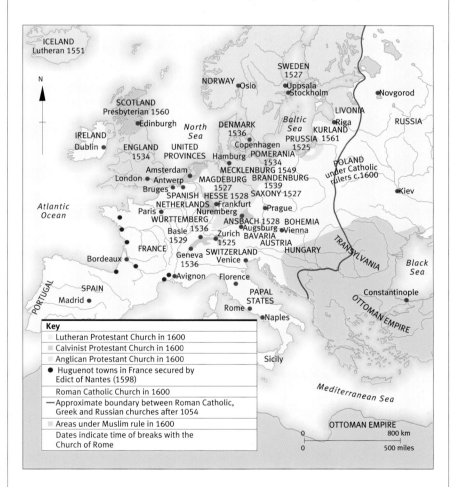

Key
- Lutheran Protestant Church in 1600
- Calvinist Protestant Church in 1600
- Anglican Protestant Church in 1600
- ● Huguenot towns in France secured by Edict of Nantes (1598)
- Roman Catholic Church in 1600
- — Approximate boundary between Roman Catholic, Greek and Russian churches after 1054
- Areas under Muslim rule in 1600
- Dates indicate time of breaks with the Church of Rome

result was somewhat to accentuate the intransigence of the Council's decisions. They not only became the touchstone of orthodoxy in doctrine and discipline until the nineteenth century, providing a standard to which Catholic rulers could rally, but also initiated

From the Venetian school of painting, this 16th-century work depicts one of the sessions of the Council of Trent. Hopes that in this general council of the Roman Catholic Church a compromise acceptable to all Christians would be reached were quickly thwarted.

institutional change. Bishops were given more authority and parishes took on new importance. More remarkably still (though almost unnoticed), it answered by implication an old question about the headship of Catholic Europe; from this time, it indisputably lay with the Pope. Like the Reformation, the Counter-Reformation went beyond forms and legal principles. It expressed and gave direction to a new devotional intensity and rejuvenated the fervour of laity and clergy alike. It made attendance at mass each week obligatory and regulated baptism and marriage more strictly; it also ended the selling of indulgences by "pardoners" – the very practice which had detonated the Lutheran explosion.

THE JESUITS

Papal authority was not the only source of Catholic reform nor was the Counter-Reformation just a response to the Protestant challenge. The spirituality and spontaneous fervour already apparent among the faithful in the fifteenth century lay behind it, too. One of the most potent expressions of its spirituality, as well as an institution which was to prove enduring was the invention of a Spaniard, the soldier Ignatius Loyola. By a curious irony he had been a student at the same Paris college as Calvin in the early 1530s, but it is not recorded that they ever met. In 1534 he and a few companions took vows; their aim was missionary work and as they trained for it Loyola devised a rule for a new religious order. In 1540 it was recognized by the pope and named the Society of Jesus. The Jesuits, as they soon came to be called, were to have an importance in the history of the Church akin to that of the early Benedictines or the Franciscans of the thirteenth century. Their warrior-founder liked to think of them as the militia of the Church, utterly disciplined and completely subordinate to papal authority through their general, who lived in Rome. They transformed Catholic education. They were in the forefront of a renewed missionary effort which carried their members to every part of the world. In Europe their intellectual eminence and political skill raised them to high places in the courts of kings.

ROMAN CATHOLIC SPAIN

THOUGH IT BROUGHT new instruments to the support of papal authority, the Counter-Reformation (like the Reformation) could also strengthen the authority of lay rulers over their subjects. The new dependence of religion upon political authority – that is to say, upon organized force – further extended the grip of the political apparatus. This was most obvious in the Spanish kingdoms. Here two forces ran together to create an unimpeachably Catholic monarchy long before the Council of Trent. The Reconquest so recently completed had been a crusade; the

title of the Catholic Monarchs itself proclaimed the identification of a political process with an ideological struggle. Secondly, the Spanish monarchy had the problem of absorbing suddenly great numbers of non-Christian subjects, both Muslims and Jews. They were feared as a potential threat to security in a multiracial society. The instrument deployed against them was a new one: an Inquisition not, like its medieval forerunner, under clerical control, but under that of the Crown. Established by papal bull in 1478, the Spanish Inquisition began to operate in Castile in 1480. The pope soon had misgivings; in Catalonia lay and ecclesiastical authority alike resisted, but to no avail. By 1516, when Charles I, the first ruler to hold both the thrones of Aragon and

The Spanish soldier Ignatius de Loyola founded the Society of Jesus, which was the Catholic Church's most effective intellectual weapon against the Protestants. The Jesuits became university professors, advisers to popes, and confessors of princes and missionaries.

Castile, became king, the Inquisition was the only institution in the Spanish domains which, from a royal council, exercised authority in all of them, in the Americas, Sicily and Sardinia as much as in Castile and Aragon. The most striking effects had already been the expulsion from them of the Jews and a severe regulation of the Moriscoes or converted Moors.

This gave Spain a religious unity unbreakable by a handful of Lutherans with whom the Inquisition found it easy to deal. The cost to Spain was in the end to be heavy. Yet already under Charles, a fervent Catholic, Spain was, in religion as in her secular life, aspiring to a new kind of centralized, absolutist monarchy, the Renaissance State par excellence, in fact. The residues of formal constitutionalism within the peninsula hardly affected this. Spain was a model for Counter-Reformation states elsewhere and one to be imposed upon much of Europe by force or example in the century after 1558, when Charles died after a retirement spent largely at his devotions in a remote monastery in Estremadura.

PHILIP II OF SPAIN

Of all the European monarchs who identified themselves with the cause of the Counter-Reformation and saw themselves as extirpators of heresy, none was more determined – and bigoted – than Charles I's son and successor, Philip II of Spain, widower of Mary Tudor. To him had come half Charles' empire: Spain, the Indies, Sicily and the Spanish Netherlands. (In 1581 he acquired Portugal, too, and it remained Spanish until 1640.) The results of his policies of religious purification in Spain have been variously interpreted. What is not open to dispute is the effect in the Spanish Netherlands, where they provoked the emergence of the first state in the world to break away from the old domination of monarchy and landed nobility.

THE REVOLT OF THE NETHERLANDS

WHAT SOME CALL the "Revolt of the Netherlands" and the Dutch call the "Eighty Years' War" has been, like many other events at the roots of nations, a great source of myth-making, some of it conscious. Even this, though, may have been less misleading than the assumption that because in the end a very modern sort of society emerged, it was a very "modern" sort of revolt, dominated by a passionate struggle for religious toleration and national independence. Nothing was less true. The troubles of the Netherlands arose in a very medieval setting, the Old Burgundian inheritance of the lands of the richest state in northern Europe, the duchy which had passed to the Habsburgs by marriage. The Spanish Netherlands, seventeen provinces of very different sorts, formed part of it. The southern provinces, where many of the inhabitants spoke French, included the most urbanized part of Europe and the great Flemish commercial centre of Antwerp. They had long been troublesome and the Flemish towns had at one moment in the late fifteenth century seemed to be trying to turn themselves into independent city-states. The northern provinces were more agricultural and maritime. Their inhabitants showed a peculiarly tenacious feeling for their land, perhaps because they had actually been recovering it from the sea and making polders since the twelfth century.

North and South were to be the later Netherlands and Belgium, but this was inconceivable in 1554. Nor could a religious division between the two be then envisaged. Though the Catholic majority of the south grew somewhat as many Protestants emigrated northwards, the two persuasions were mixed upon both sides of a future boundary. Early sixteenth-century Europe was much more tolerant of religious divisions than it would be after the Counter-Reformation got to work.

Philip's determination to enforce the decrees of the Council of Trent explains something of what followed but the origins of trouble went back a long way. As the Spaniards strove to modernize the relations of central government and local communities, they did so with more up-to-date methods and perhaps less tact than the Burgundians

This allegory of the tyranny of the Spanish Duke of Alva (c.1600) was painted to justify the Dutch rebellion against Spanish rule. Alva, who has enchained figures representing the Dutch provinces, is shown being crowned by the devil, while outside the executions of the counts Egmont and Horn, condemned to death by the duke, are carried out.

had shown. Spanish royal envoys came into conflict first with the nobility of the southern provinces. As prickly and touchy as other nobilities of the age in defence of their symbolic "liberties" – that is, privileges and immunities – they felt threatened by a monarch more remote than the great Charles who, they felt, had understood them (he spoke their language), even if he was Charles' son. The Spanish commander, the Duke of Alva, they argued, was further violating local privilege by interfering with local jurisdictions in the pursuit of heretics. Catholic though they were, they had a stake in the prosperity of the Flemish cities where Protestantism had taken root and feared the introductions to them of the Spanish Inquisition. They were, too, as uneasy as other noblemen of the times about the pressures of inflation.

their number, William, Prince of Orange, united the nobles against their lawful ruler. Like his contemporary, Elizabeth Tudor, William (nicknamed the "Silent" because of his reputed refusal to allow unguarded anger to escape him when he learnt of his ruler's determination to bring his heretic subjects to heel) was good at suggesting sympathy for popular causes. But there was always a potential rift between noblemen and Calvinist townsmen who had more at stake. Better political tactics by Spanish governors and the victories of the Spanish armies were in the end enough to force it open. The nobles fell back into line and thus, without knowing it, the Spanish armies defined modern Belgium. The struggle continued only in the northern provinces (though still under the political direction of William the Silent until his murder in 1584).

WILLIAM THE SILENT

Resistance to Spanish government began in thoroughly medieval forms, in the Estates of Brabant, and for a few years the brutality of the Spanish army and the leadership of one of

THE NEW DUTCH NATION

The Dutch (as we may now call them) had much at stake and were not encumbered as their southern co-religionists had been with the ambiguous dissatisfactions of the nobility.

But they were divided among themselves; the provinces could rarely come easily to agreement. On the other hand, they could use the cry of religious freedom and a broad toleration to disguise their divisions. They benefited, too, from a great migration northward of Flemish capital and talent. Their enemies had difficulties; the Spanish army was formidable but could not easily deal with an enemy which retired behind its town walls and surrounded them with water by opening the dykes and flooding the countryside. The Dutch, almost by accident, transferred their main effort to the sea where they could do a great deal of damage to the Spanish on more equal terms. Spanish communications with the Netherlands were more difficult once the northern sea route was harried by the rebels. It was expensive to maintain a big army in Belgium by the long road up from Italy and even more expensive when other enemies had to be beaten off. That was soon the case. The Counter-Reformation had infected international politics with a new ideological element. Together with their interest in maintaining a balance of power on the continent and preventing the complete success of the Spanish, this led the English first to a diplomatic and then to a military and naval struggle against Spain which brought the Dutch allies.

The war created, almost fortuitously and incidentally, a remarkable new society, a loose federation of seven little republics with a weak central government, called the United Provinces. Soon, its citizens discovered a forgotten national past (much as decolonized Africans have done in this century) and celebrated the virtues of Germanic tribesmen dimly discernible in Roman accounts of rebellion; relics of their enthusiasm remain in the paintings commissioned by Amsterdam magnates depicting attacks upon Roman camps (this was in the era we remember for the work of Rembrandt). The distinctiveness of a new

William the Silent, Prince of Orange (1533–1584), the leader of the revolt against the Duke of Alva's régime in the Netherlands, is depicted in this 19th-century wall painting. William, who was born a Catholic, converted to Protestantism during his exile in Germany (1567–1572), and was known for his religious tolerance.

nation thus consciously created is now more interesting than such historical propaganda. Once survival was assured, the United Provinces enjoyed religious tolerance, great civic freedom and provincial independence; the Dutch did not allow Calvinism the upper hand in government.

ELIZABETHAN ENGLAND

Later generations came to think they saw a similar linkage of religious and civic freedom in Elizabethan England; this was anachronistic, although comprehensible given the way English institutions were to evolve over the next century or so. Paradoxically, one part of this was a great strengthening of the legislative authority of the state, one which carried the limitation of privilege so far that at the end of the seventeenth century it was

Elizabeth I (1533–1603) reigned as Queen of England at a time when her country was emerging as a world power. She skilfully maintained the unity of her realm in the face of attack by the Spanish Armada and threats to her own life by Catholic supporters of her cousin Mary Stuart. Her image as the "Virgin Queen" was carefully preserved by her portrait painters; throughout her long reign, she was consistently depicted in flattering terms.

regarded with amazement by other Europeans. For a long time this cannot have seemed a likely outcome. Elizabeth had been an incomparable producer of the royal spectacle. When the myths of beauty and youth faded she had acquired the majesty of those who outlive their early counsellors. In 1603 she had been queen for forty-five years, the centre of a national cult fed by her own Tudor instinct for welding the dynasty's interest to patriotism, by poets of genius, by mundane devices such as the frequent travel (which kept down expenses, since she stayed with her nobility) which made her visible to her people, and by her astonishing skill with her parliaments. Nor did she persecute for religion's sake; she did not, as she put it, want to make "windows into men's souls". It is hardly surprising that the accession day of Good Queen Bess became a festival of patriotic opposition to government under her successors. Unhappily, she had no child to whom to bequeath the glamour she brought to monarchy, and she left an encumbered estate. Like all other rulers of her day, she never had a big enough income. The inheritance of debt did not help the first king of the Scottish house of Stuart, who succeeded her, James I. The shortcomings of the males of that dynasty are still difficult to write about with moderation; the Stuarts gave England four bad kings in a row. Still, James was neither as foolish as his son nor as unprincipled as his grandsons. It was probably his lack of tact and alien ways rather than more serious defects that did most to embitter politics in his reign.

In defence of the Stuarts, it can be agreed that this was not the only troubled monarchy. In the seventeenth century there was a roughly contemporaneous crisis of authority in several countries, and one curiously parallel to an economic crisis which was Europe-wide. The two may have been con-nected, but it is not easy to be sure what the nature of the connexion was. It is also interesting that these civil struggles coincided with the last phase of a period of religious wars which had been opened by the Counter-Reformation. We may at least assume that a contemporaneous breakdown of normal political life in a number of countries, notably England, France and Spain, owed something to the needs of governments forced to take part in them.

CIVIL WAR IN ENGLAND

In England the crisis came to a head in civil war, regicide and the establishment of the

The reign of James VI (1566–1625), King of Scotland from 1567 and of Great Britain and Ireland (as James I) from 1603, was dogged by financial crises, struggles between Protestant, Puritan and Catholic factions in both of his kingdoms, and clashes with Parliament.

Charles I (1600–1649), King of Great Britain and Ireland, is depicted in a portrait after Sir Anthony van Dyck, the Flemish painter who was knighted by the king. Charles I was tried for treason after his supporters were defeated in the second phase of the English Civil War in 1648. He refused to plead at his trial, claiming that the court was illegitimate, and was condemned to death by beheading. He is remembered for the great courage and dignity with which he died.

only republic in English history. Historians still argue about where lay the heart of the quarrel and the point of no return in what became armed conflict between Charles I and his parliament. One crucial moment came when he found himself at war with one set of his subjects (for he was King of Scotland, as well as England), and had to call Parliament to help him in 1640. Without new taxation, England could not be defended. But by then some of its members were convinced that there was a royal scheme to overturn from within the Church by law established and reintroduce the power of Rome. Parliament harried the king's servants (sending the two most conspicuous to the block). Charles decided in 1642 that force was the only way out and so the Civil War began. In it he was defeated. Parliament was uneasy, as were all the English, for if you stepped outside the ancient constitution of King, Lords and Commons, where would things end? But Charles threw away his advantage by seeking a foreign invasion in his support (the Scots were to fight for him, this time). Those who dominated Parliament had had enough and Charles was tried and executed. His son went into exile.

THE ENGLISH REPUBLIC

AFTER THE EXECUTION of Charles I, there followed in England an interregnum during which the dominant figure, until his death in 1658, was one of the most remarkable of all Englishmen, Oliver Cromwell. He was a country gentleman who had risen in the parliamentary side's councils by his genius as a soldier. This gave him great power, for provided his army stood by him he could dispense with the politicians, but also imposed limitations on him, for he could not risk losing the army's support. The result was an English republic astonishingly fertile in new constitutional schemes, as Oliver cast about to find a way of governing through Parliament without delivering England to an intolerant Protestantism. This was the Commonwealth.

PURITANISM

The intolerance of some parliamentarians was one expression of a many-sided strain in English (and American) Protestantism which has been named Puritanism. It was an ill-defined but growing force in English life since Elizabeth's reign. Its spokesmen had originally sought only a particularly close and austere interpretation of religious doctrine and ceremony. There were Puritans inside the Anglican Church as well as among the critics who were impatient over its retention of much from the Catholic past, but it was to this second tendency that the name was more and more applied. By the seventeenth century the epithet "puritan" also betokened, besides rigid doctrine and disapproval of ritual, the reform of manners in a strongly Calvinistic sense. By the time of the republic, many who had been on the parliament's side in the Civil War appeared to wish to use its victory to impose Puritanism, both doctrinal and moral, by law not only on conservative and royalist Anglicans, but on dissenting religious minorities – Congregationalists, Baptists, Unitarians – which had found their voice under the Commonwealth. There was nothing politically or religiously democratic about Puritanism. Those who were of the Elect might freely choose their own elders and act as a self-governing community, but from

outside the self-designated circle of the saved they looked (and were) an oligarchy claiming to know God's will for others, and therefore all the more unacceptable. It was a few, untypical minorities, not the dominant Protestant establishment, which threw up the democratic and levelling ideas which contributed so much to the great debate of the republican years.

THE RESTORATION OF THE ENGLISH MONARCHY

The publication of more than twenty thousand books and pamphlets on political and religious issues would by itself have made the Civil War and Commonwealth years a great epoch in English political education. Unfortunately, once Oliver had died, the institutional bankruptcy of the republic was clear. The English could not agree in sufficient numbers to uphold any new constitution. But most of them, it turned

This 17th-century painting portrays Oliver Cromwell (1599–1658) who, after the abolition of the monarchy, the House of Lords, the bishops and finally the House of Commons (1653), ruled as Lord Protector of England and the Commonwealth.

Charles II, son of the executed Charles I, was crowned king in Scotland in 1651, but spent nine years in exile in the aftermath of the Civil War. He returned to England in triumph in 1660, when the monarchy was restored.

out, would accept the old device of monarchy. So the story of the Commonwealth ended with the restoration of the Stuarts in 1660. England in fact had her king back on unspoken conditions: in the last resort, Charles II came back because Parliament said so, and believed he would defend the Church of England. Counter-Reformation Catholicism frightened the English as much as did revolutionary Puritanism. Although the struggle of monarch and Parliament was not over, there would be no absolute monarchy in England; henceforth the Crown was on the defensive.

Historians have tried to see much more than this in so great an episode of English history and have argued lengthily about what the so-called "English Revolution" expressed. Clearly, religion played a big part in it. Extreme Protestantism was given a chance to have an influence on the national life it was never again to have; this earned it the deep dislike of the Church of England and made political England anti-clerical for centuries. It was not without cause that the best English historian of the struggle has spoken of the "Puritan Revolution". But religion no more exhausts the meaning of these years than does the constitutional quarrel. Others have sought a class struggle in the Civil War. Of the interested motives of many of those engaged there can be no doubt, but it does not fit any clear general pattern. Still others have seen a struggle between a swollen "Court", a governmental nexus of bureaucrats, courtiers and politicians, all linked to the system by financial dependence upon it, and "Country", the local notables who paid for this. But localities often divided: it was one of the tragedies of the Civil War that even families could be split by it. It remains easier to be clear about the results of the English Revolution than about its origins or meaning.

FRANCE UNDER CARDINAL RICHELIEU

Most continental countries were appalled by the trial and execution of Charles I, but they had their own bloody troubles. A period of conscious assertion of royal power in France by Cardinal Richelieu not only reduced the privileges of the Huguenots (as French Calvinists had come to be called) but had installed royal officials in the provinces as the direct representatives of royal power; these were the intendants. Administrative reform was an aggravation of the almost continuous suffering of the French people in the 1630s and 1640s. In the still overwhelmingly agricultural economy of France, Richelieu's measures were bound to hurt the poor most. Taxes on the peasant doubled and sometimes trebled in a few years. An eruption of popular rebellion, mercilessly repressed, was the result. Some parts of France, moreover, were devastated by the campaigns of the last phase of the great struggle for Germany and central Europe called the Thirty Years' War, the phase in which it became a Bourbon-Habsburg conflict. Lorraine, Burgundy and much of eastern France were reduced to ruins, the population of some areas declining by a quarter or a third. The claim that the French monarchy sought to impose new and (some said) unconstitutional taxation finally detonated political crisis under Richelieu's successors. The role of defender of the traditional constitution was taken up by special interests, notably the *parlement* of Paris, the corporation of lawyers who sat in and could plead before the first law court of the kingdom. In 1648 they led an insurrection in Paris (soon named the Fronde). A compromise settlement was followed after an uneasy interval by a second, much more dangerous Fronde, led this time by great noblemen. Though the *parlement* of Paris did not long maintain a united front with them, these men could draw on the anti-centralist feelings of the provincial nobility, as regional rebellions showed. Yet the Crown survived (and so did the intendants). In 1660 the absolute monarchy of France was still essentially intact.

CIVIC UNREST IN THE RENAISSANCE STATES

In Spain, too, taxation provoked troubles. An attempt by a minister to overcome the provincialism inherent in the formally federal structure of the Spanish state led to revolt in Portugal (which had been absorbed into Spain with promises of respect for her liberties from Philip II), among the Basques and in Catalonia. The last was to take twelve years to suppress. There was also a revolt in 1647 in the Spanish kingdom of Naples.

In all these instances of civic turbulence, demands for money provoked resistance. In the financial sense, then, the Renaissance State was far from successful. The appearance of standing armies in most states in the seventeenth century did not mark only a military revolution. War was a great devourer of taxes. Yet the burdens of taxation laid on the French seem far greater than those laid on the English: why, then, did the French monarchy appear to suffer less from the "crisis"? England, on the other hand, had civil war and the overthrow (for a time) of her monarchy without the devastation which went with foreign invasion. Nor were her occasional riots over high prices to be compared with the appalling bloodshed of the peasant risings of seventeenth-century France. In England, too,

Cardinal Richelieu (1585–1642), principal minister to King Louis XIII of France, was a great promoter of the absolute authority of the state and the founder of a French national foreign policy.

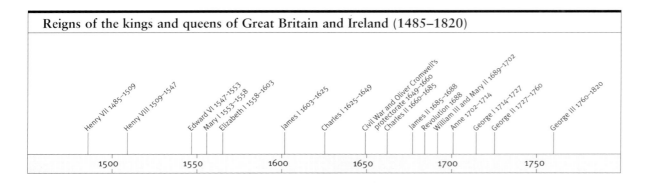

Reigns of the kings and queens of Great Britain and Ireland (1485–1820)

Henry VII 1485–1509
Henry VIII 1509–1547
Edward VI 1547–1553
Mary I 1553–1558
Elizabeth I 1558–1603
James I 1603–1625
Charles I 1625–1649
Civil War and Oliver Cromwell's protectorate 1649–1660
Charles II 1660–1685
James II 1685–1688
Revolution 1688
William III and Mary II 1689–1702
Anne 1702–1714
George I 1714–1727
George II 1727–1760
George III 1760–1820

1500   1550   1600   1650   1700   1750

Free food is distributed to victims of the Frondes at the gates of a Parisian abbey, depicted in an 18th-century watercolour from the French school.

there was a specific challenge to authority from religious dissent. In Spain this was non-existent and in France it had been contained long before. The Huguenots, indeed, were a vested interest; but they saw their protector in the monarchy and therefore rallied to it in the Frondes. Regionalism was important in Spain, to a smaller extent in France where it provided a foothold for conservative interests threatened by governmental innovation, but seems to have played very little part in England.

The year 1660, when the young Louis XIV assumed full powers in France and Charles II returned to England, was, in fact, something of a turning-point. France was not to prove ungovernable again until 1789 and was to show, in the next half-century, astonishing military and diplomatic power. In England there was never again to be, in spite of further constitutional troubles and the deposition of another king, a civil war. The last English rebellion, by an inadequate pretender and a few thousand deluded yokels in 1685, in no sense menaced the state. After 1660 there was an English standing army, after all. This makes it all the more striking, in retrospect, that people remained so unwilling to admit the reality of sovereignty. The English solemnly legislated a series of defences of individual liberty in the Bill of Rights, yet even in 1689 it was hard to argue that what one king in Parliament had done, another could not undo. In France everyone agreed the king's power was absolute, yet lawyers went on saying that there were things he could not legally do.

HOBBES

One thinker at least, the greatest of English political philosophers, Thomas Hobbes, showed in his books, notably in the *Leviathan* of 1651, that he recognized the way society was moving. Hobbes argued that the disadvantages and uncertainties of not agreeing that someone should have the last word in deciding what was law clearly outweighed the danger that such power might be tyrannically employed. The troubles of his times deeply impressed him with the need to know certainly where authority was to be found. Even when they were not continuous, disorders were always liable to break out: as Hobbes put it (roughly), you do not have to live all the time under a torrential downpour to say that the weather is rainy. The recognition that legislative power – sovereignty – rested, limitless, in the state and not elsewhere, and that it could not be restricted by appeals to immunities, customs, divine law or anything else without the danger of falling into anarchy, was Hobbes' contribution to political theory, though he got small thanks for it and had to wait until the nineteenth century for due recognition. Though, in practice, people often acted as though they accepted his views, he was almost universally condemned.

Hobbes' *Leviathan*

"The finall Cause, End, or Designe of men (who naturally love Liberty, and Dominion over others), in the introduction of that restraint upon themselves (in which wee see them live in Commonwealths) is the foresight of their own preservation ... that is to say, of getting themselves out from that miserable condition of Warre, which is necessarily consequent ... to the naturall Passions of men, when there is no visible Power to keep them in awe, and tye them by feare of punishment to the performance of their Covenants, and observation of those Lawes of Nature ... .

For the Lawes of Nature (as *Justice, Equity, Modesty, Mercy*, and (in summe) *doing to others, as wee would be done to*,) of themselves, without the terrour of some Power, to cause them to be observed, are contrary to our naturall Passions, that carry us to Partiality, Pride, Revenge, and the like."

An extract from Chap. 17, Part II ("Of Commonwealth") of the *Leviathan* by Thomas Hobbes, 1651, edited by C. B. Macpherson.

CONSTITUTIONAL ENGLAND

Constitutional England was in fact one of the first states to operate on Hobbes' principles. By the early eighteenth century, the English (the Scotch were less sure, even when they came under the parliament at Westminster after the Act of Union of 1707) accepted in principle and sometimes showed in practice that there could be no limits except practical ones to the potential scope of law. This conclusion was to be explicitly challenged even as late as Victorian times, but was implicit when in 1688 England at last rejected the direct descent of the Stuart male line, pushed James II off the throne and put his daughter and her consort on it on conditions. With the creation of a contractual monarchy England at last broke with her *ancien régime* and began to function as a constitutional state. Effectively, centralized power was shared; its major component lay with a House of Commons which represented the dominant social interest, the landowning classes. The king still kept important powers of his own but his advisers, it soon became clear, must possess the confidence of the House of Commons. The legislative sovereign, the Crown in Parliament, could do anything by statute. No

This was the title page for the first edition of the *Leviathan* by the English philosopher Thomas Hobbes (1588–1679).

such immunity as still protected privilege in continental countries existed. The English answer to the danger posed by such a concentration of authority was to secure, by revolution if necessary, that the authority should only act in accordance with the wishes of the most important elements in society.

THE "GLORIOUS REVOLUTION" OF 1688

The year 1688 gave England a Dutch king, Queen Mary's husband, William III, to whom the major importance of the "Glorious Revolution" of that year was that England could be mobilized against France, now threatening the independence of the United Provinces. There were too many complicated interests at work in them for the Anglo-French wars which followed to be interpreted in merely constitutional or ideological terms. Moreover, the presence of the Holy Roman Empire, Spain and various German princes in the shifting anti-French coalitions of the next quarter-century would certainly make nonsense of any neat contrast of political principle between the two sides. Nevertheless, it rightly struck some contemporaries that there was an ideological element buried somewhere in the struggle. England and Holland were more open societies than the France of Louis XIV. They allowed and protected the exercise of different religions. They did not censor the press but left it to be regulated by the laws which protected persons and the state against defamation. They were governed by oligarchies representing the effective possessors of social and economic power. France was at the opposite pole.

LOUIS XIV

UNDER LOUIS XIV, absolute government reached its climax in France. It is not easy to pin his ambitions down in familiar categories; for him personal, dynastic and national greatness were hardly distinguishable. Perhaps that is why he became a model for all European princes. Politics was reduced effectively to administration; the royal councils, together with the royal agents in the provinces, the intendants and military commanders, took due account of such social facts as the existence of the nobility and local immunities, but the reign played havoc with the real independence of the political forces so powerful hitherto in France. This was the era of the establishment of royal power throughout the country and some later saw it as a revolutionary one; in the second half of the century the frame which Richelieu had knocked together was at last filled up by administrative reality. Louis XIV tamed

This 17th-century engraving depicts the coronation of William III and Mary II, which took place in 1689.

aristocrats by offering them the most glamorous court in Europe; his own sense of social hierarchy made him happy to caress them with honours and pensions, but he never forgot the Frondes and controlled the nobility as had Richelieu. Louis' relatives were excluded from his council, which contained non-noble ministers on whom he could safely rely. The *parlements* were restricted to their judicial role; the French Church's independence of Roman authority was asserted, but only to bring it the more securely under the wing of the Most Christian King (as one of Louis' titles had it). As for the Huguenots, Louis was determined, whatever the cost, not to be a ruler of heretics; those who were not exiled were submitted to a harsh persecution to bring them to conversion.

THE PERFECT ABSOLUTE MONARCHY

The coincidence with a great age of French cultural achievement seems to make it hard for the French to recognize the harsh face of the reign of Louis XIV. He ruled a hierarchical, corporate, theocratic society which, even if up-to-date in methods, looked to the past for its goals. Louis even hoped to become Holy Roman Emperor. He refused to allow Descartes, the defender of religion, to be given religious burial in France because of the dangers of his ideas. Yet for a long time his

kind of government seems to have been what most French people wanted. The process of effective government could be brutal, as Huguenots who were coerced into conversion by having soldiers billeted on them, or peasants reluctant to pay taxes who were visited by a troop of cavalry for a month or so, both knew. Yet life may have been better than life a few decades previously, in spite of some exceptionally hard years. The reign was the end of an era of disorder, not the start of one. France was largely free from invasion and there was a drop in the return expected from investment in land which lasted well into the eighteenth century. These were solid realities to underpin the glittering façade of an age later called the *Grand Siècle*.

Louis' European position was won in large measure by success in war (and by the end of the reign, he had undergone bad setbacks), but it was not only his armies and diplomacy which mattered. He carried French prestige to a peak at which it was long to remain because of the model of monarchy he presented; he was the perfect absolute monarch. The physical setting of the Ludovican achievement was the huge new palace of Versailles. Few buildings or the lives lived in them can have been so aped and imitated. In the eighteenth century Europe was to be studded with miniature reproductions of the French court, painfully created at the expense of their subjects by would-be *grands monarques* in the decades of stability

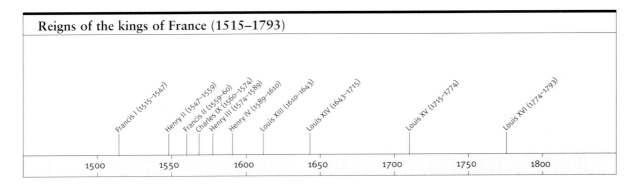

Reigns of the kings of France (1515–1793)

Francis I (1515–1547)
Henry II (1547–1559)
Francis II (1559–60)
Charles IX (1560–1574)
Henry III (1574–1589)
Henry IV (1589–1610)
Louis XIII (1610–1643)
Louis XIV (1643–1715)
Louis XV (1715–1774)
Louis XVI (1774–1793)

1500   1550   1600   1650   1700   1750   1800

This Gobelins tapestry represents the wedding ceremony of Louis XIV of France and the Infanta Maria Theresa, daughter of Philip IV of Spain, in 1660.

and continuity which almost everywhere followed the upheavals of the great wars of Louis' reign.

ENLIGHTENED DESPOTISM

THERE WERE BETWEEN 1715 and 1740 no important international tensions to provoke internal change in states, nor were there great ideological divisions such as those of the seventeenth century, nor rapid economic and social development with their consequential strain. Not surprisingly, therefore, governments changed little and everywhere society seemed to settle down after a turbulent century or so. Apart from Great Britain, the United Provinces, the cantons of Switzerland and the fossil republics of Italy, absolute monarchy was the dominant state form. It remained so for most of the eighteenth century, sometimes in a style which came to be

called "enlightened despotism" – a slippery term, which neither has nor ever had a clear meaning any more than terms like "Right" or "Left" have today. What it indicates is that from about 1750 the wish to carry out practical reforms led some rulers to innovations which seemed to be influenced by the advanced thought of the day. Such innovations, when effective, were imposed none the less by the machinery of absolute monarchical power. If sometimes humanitarian, the policies of "enlightened despots" were not necessarily politically liberal. They were, on the other hand, usually modern in that they undermined traditional social and religious authority, cut across accepted notions of social hierarchy or legal rights, and helped to concentrate lawmaking power in the state and assert its unchallenged authority over its subjects, who were treated increasingly as an aggregate of individuals rather than as members of a hierarchy of corporations.

Not surprisingly, it is almost impossible to find an example which in practice perfectly fulfils this general description, just as it is impossible to find a definition of a "democratic" state today, or a "fascist" state in the 1930s, which fits all examples. Among Mediterranean and southern countries, for example, Naples, Spain, Portugal and some other Italian states (and even at times the Papal States) had ministers who sought economic reform. Some of these were stimulated by novelty; others – Portugal and Spain – turned to enlightened despotism as a way to recover lost status as great powers. Some encroached on the powers of the Church. Almost all of them served rulers who were part of the Bourbon family connexion. The involvement of one of the smallest of them, Parma, in a quarrel with the papacy led to a general attack in all of these countries on the right arm of the Counter-Reformation papacy, the Society of Jesus. In 1773 the pope was driven by them to dissolve the Society, a great symbolic defeat, as important for its demonstration of the strength of advanced anti-clerical principles even in Catholic Europe as for its practical effects.

EASTERN EUROPEAN ABSOLUTISM

Among these states only Spain had any pretension to great power status and she was in decline. Of the eastern enlightened despotisms, on the other hand, three out of four certainly had. The odd man out was Poland, the sprawling ramshackle kingdom where reform on "enlightened" lines came to grief on constitutional rocks; the enlightenment was there all right, but not the despotism to make it effective. More successfully, Prussia, the Habsburg empire and Russia all managed to sustain a façade of enlightenment while strengthening the state. Once more, the clue

to change can be found in war, which cost far more than building even the most lavish replica of Versailles. In Russia modernization of the state went back to the earliest years of the century, when Peter the Great sought to guarantee her future as a great power through technical and institutional change. In the second half of the century, the empress Catherine II reaped many of the benefits of this. She also gave the régime a thin veneer of up-to-the-minute ideas by advertizing widely her patronage of letters and humanitarianism. This was all very superficial; the traditional ordering of society was unchanged. Russia was a conservative despotism whose politics were largely a matter of the struggles of noble factions and families. Nor did enlightenment much change things in Prussia, where there was a well-established tradition of efficient, centralized, economical administration embodying much of what reformers sought elsewhere. Prussia already enjoyed religious toleration and the Hohenzollern monarchy ruled a strongly traditional society virtually unchanged in the eighteenth century. The Prussian king was

King Philip V of Spain (1683– 1746), who is portrayed with his family in this 18th-century painting, considered himself to be an enlightened despot.

obliged to recognize – and willingly did so – that his power rested on the acquiescence of his nobles and he carefully preserved their legal and social privilege. Frederick II remained convinced that only noblemen should be given commissioned rank in his army and at the end of his reign there were more serfs in Prussian territory than there had been at the beginning.

THE HABSBURG EMPIRE

COMPETITION WITH PRUSSIA was a decisive stimulus to reform in the Habsburg dominions. There were great obstacles in the way. The dynasty's territories were very diverse, in nationality, language, institutions; the emperor was King of Hungary, Duke of Milan, Archduke of Austria, to name only a few of his many titles. Centralization and greater administrative uniformity were essential if this variegated empire was to exercise its due weight in European affairs. Another problem was that, like the Bourbon states, but unlike Russia or Prussia, the Habsburg empire was overwhelmingly Roman Catholic. Everywhere the power of the Church was deeply entrenched; the Habsburg lands included most of those outside Spain where the Counter-Reformation had been most successful. The Church also owned huge properties; it was everywhere protected by tradition, canon law and papal policy, and it had a monopoly of education. Finally, the Habsburgs provided almost without interruption during these centuries the successive occupants of the throne of the Holy Roman Empire. In consequence they had special responsibilities in Germany.

Catherine II of Russia (1729–1796), portrayed in this 18th-century engraving, imposed the French language, customs and fashions on her court. With the support of the nobility, the great tsarina also had complete control of the Russian state.

HABSBURG REFORM

This background was always likely to give modernization in the Habsburg dominions an "enlightened" colour. Everywhere practical reform seemed to conflict with entrenched social power or the Church. The empress Maria Theresia was herself by no means sympathetic to reform which had such implications, but her advisers were able to present a persuasive case for it when, after the 1740s, it became clear that the Habsburg monarchy would have to struggle for supremacy with Prussia. Once the road to fiscal and consequently administrative reform had been entered upon, it was in the end bound to lead to conflict between Church and State. This came to a climax in the reign of Maria Theresia's son and successor, Joseph II, a man who did not share the pieties of his mother and who was alleged to have advanced views. His reforms became especially associated with measures of secularization. Monasteries lost their property, religious appointments were interfered with, the right of sanctuary was removed and education was taken out of the hands of the clergy. So far as it went, this awoke angry opposition, but mattered less than the fact that by 1790 Joseph had antagonized to the point of open defiance the nobles of Brabant, Hungary and Bohemia. The powerful local institutions – estates and diets – through which those lands could oppose his policies paralysed government in many of Joseph's realms at the end of his reign.

RESISTANCE TO FRENCH REFORM

Differences in the circumstances in which they were applied, in the preconceptions which governed them, in the success they

achieved and in the degree to which they did or did not embody "enlightened" ideas, all show how misleading is any idea that there was, anywhere, a "typical" enlightened despotism to serve as a model. The government of France, clearly touched by reforming policies and aspirations, only confirms this. Obstacles to change had, paradoxically, grown stronger after the death of Louis XIV. Under his successor (whose reign began with a minority under a regent), the real influence of the privileged had grown and increasingly there grew up in the *parlements* a tendency to criticize laws which infringed special interest and historic privilege. There was a new and growing resistance to the idea that there rested in the Crown any right of unrestricted legislative sovereignty. As the century wore on, France's international role imposed

Frederick II of Prussia (1712–1786), known as Frederick the Great, called himself "the first servant of the state", a phrase which was quickly adopted in other royal circles.

heavier and heavier burdens on her finances and the issue of reform tended to crystallize in the issue of finding new tax revenue – an exercise that was bound to bring on conflicts. Onto this rock ran most of the proposals for reform within the French monarchy.

Paradoxically, France was in 1789 the country most associated with the articulation and diffusion of critical and advanced ideas, yet also one of those where it seemed most difficult to put them into practice. But this was an issue which was Europe-wide in the traditional monarchies of the end of the eighteenth century. Wherever reform and modernization had been tried, the hazards of vested historical interest and traditional social structure threw obstacles in the way. In the last resort, it was unlikely that monarchical absolutism could have solved this problem anywhere. It could not question historical authority too closely for this was what it rested upon itself. Unrestricted legislative sovereignty seemed still in the eighteenth century to call too much in question. If historic rights were infringed, could not property be? This was a fair point, though Europe's most successful ruling class, the English, seemed to accept that nothing was outside the sphere of legislative competence, nothing beyond the scope of reform, without fears that such a revolutionary idea was likely to be used against them.

almost always proved temporary. True, even the most determined reformers and the ablest statesmen had to work with a machinery of state which to any modern bureaucrat would seem woefully inadequate. Though the eighteenth-century state might mobilize resources much greater than had done its predecessors it had to do so with no revolutionary innovations of technique. Communications in 1800 depended just as they had done in 1500 on wind and muscle; the "telegraph" which came into use in the 1790s was only a semaphore system, worked by pulling ropes. Armies could move only slightly faster than three centuries earlier, and if their weapons were improved, they were not improved out of recognition. No police force such as exists today existed in any country; income tax lay still in the future. The change in the power of the state came about because of changes in ideas and because of the development to greater efficiency of well-known institutions, rather than because of technology. In no major state before 1789 could it even be assumed that all its subjects would understand the language of government, while none, except perhaps Great Britain and the United Provinces, succeeded in so identifying itself with its subjects as to leave its government more concerned to protect them against foreigners than itself against them.

THE GROWTH OF STATE POWER

With this important qualification, though, enlightened despotism, too, embodies the theme already set out – that at the heart of the complex story of political evolution in many countries over a period of three centuries, continuity lies in the growth of the power of the state. The occasional successes of those who tried to put the clock back

E mpress Maria Theresia (1717–1780), the daughter of the emperor Charles VI, was Archduchess of Austria and Queen of Hungary and Bohemia from 1740. Her husband, Francis I, became Holy Roman Emperor in 1745, and her eldest son, Joseph II, succeeded him in 1765. One of her daughters, Marie Antoinette, was married to the future French king Louis XVI in 1770.

3 THE NEW WORLD OF GREAT POWERS

AMONG THE INSTITUTIONS which took their basic shape in the fifteenth and sixteenth centuries and are still with us today are those of formal diplomacy. Rulers had sent messages to one another and negotiated, but there were always many ways of doing this and of understanding what was going on. The Chinese, for example, used the fiction that their emperor was ruler of the world and that all embassies to him were therefore of the nature of petitions or tributes by subjects. Medieval kings had sent one another heralds, about whom a special ceremonial had grown up and whom special rules protected, or occasional missions of ambassadors. After 1500, it slowly became the practice to use in peacetime the standard device we still employ, of a permanently resident ambassador through whom all ordinary business is at least initially transacted and who has the task of keeping his own rulers informed about the country to which he is accredited.

THE NEW DIPLOMATIC SYSTEM

The first notable examples of permanent ambassadors were Venetian. It is not surprising that a republic so dependent on trade and the maintenance of regular relationships should have provided the first examples of the professional diplomat. More changes followed. Gradually, the hazards of the life of earlier emissaries were forgotten as diplomats were given a special status protected by privileges and immunities. The nature of treaties and other diplomatic forms also became more precise and regularized. Procedure became more standardized. All these changes came about slowly, when they were believed to be useful. For the most part, it is true, the professional diplomat in the modern sense had not yet appeared by 1800, ambassadors were

This 15th-century painting depicts the emperor Maximilian (1459–1519) and his family. The Habsburgs' diplomatic and matrimonial policies turned the House of Austria into a major European force and eventually resulted in the division of the dynasty into two branches – Spanish and Austrian.

then still usually noblemen who could afford to sustain a representative role, not paid civil servants. None the less, the professionalization of diplomacy was beginning. It is another sign that after 1500 a new world of relationships between sovereign powers was replacing that of feudal ties between persons and the vague supremacies of pope and emperor.

The most striking characteristic of this new system is the assumption that the world is divided into sovereign states. This idea took time to emerge; sixteenth-century Europe was certainly not seen by contemporaries as a set of independent areas, each governed by a ruler of its own, belonging to it alone. Still less were its components thought to have in any but a few cases any sort of unity which might be called "national". That this was so was not only because of the survival of such museums of past practice as the Holy Roman Empire. It was also because the dominating principle of early modern Europe's diplomacy was dynasticism.

DYNASTICISM

In the sixteenth and seventeenth centuries, the political units of Europe were less states than landed estates. They were accumulations of property put together over long or short periods by aggressiveness, marriage and inheritance – by the same processes and forces, that is to say, by which any private family's estate might be built up. The results were to be seen on maps whose boundaries continually changed as this or that portion of an inheritance passed from one ruler to another. The inhabitants had no more say in the matter than might the peasants living on a farm which changed hands. Dynasticism accounts for the monotonous preoccupation of negotiations and treaty-making with the possible consequences of marriages and the careful establishment and scrutiny of lines of succession.

Besides their dynastic interests, rulers also argued and fought about religion, and, increasingly, trade or wealth. Some of them acquired overseas possessions; this, too, became a complicating factor. Occasionally, the old principles of feudal superiority might still be invoked. There were also always map-making forces at work which fell outside the operation of these principles, such as settlement of new land or a rising national sentiment. Nevertheless, broadly speaking, most rulers in the sixteenth and seventeenth centuries saw themselves as the custodians of inherited rights and interests which they had to pass on. In this they behaved as was expected; they mirrored the attitudes of other men and other families in their societies. It was not only the Middle Ages which were fascinated by lineage, and the sixteenth and seventeenth centuries were the great age of genealogy.

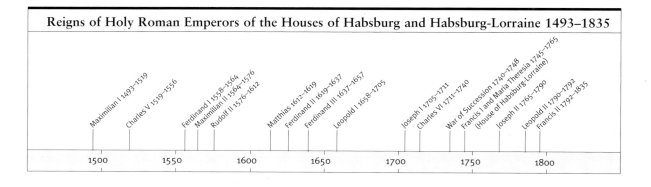

Reigns of Holy Roman Emperors of the Houses of Habsburg and Habsburg-Lorraine 1493–1835

The Catholic Monarchs in Spain, like most royal European dynasties, used marriage as a means of extending their rule. Isabella of Castile and Ferdinand II of Aragon arranged a double marriage with the House of Austria: that of John with Marguerite and that of their daughter the Infanta Joanna with Philip I, known as the Handsome. The latter couple, depicted on these 16th-century panels, had two sons (later the emperors Charles V and Ferdinand I), who inherited a vast empire.

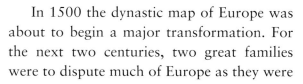

In 1500 the dynastic map of Europe was about to begin a major transformation. For the next two centuries, two great families were to dispute much of Europe as they were already at that date disputing Italy. These were the house of Habsburg and the ruling house of France, first Valois, then after the accession of Henry IV in 1589, Bourbon. The one would come to be predominantly Austrian and the other's centre would always be France. But both would export rulers and consorts of rulers to many other countries. The heart of their quarrel when the sixteenth century began was the Burgundian inheritance. Each of them was then far from playing a wider European role. Indeed, there was not a great deal to distinguish them at that date in power – though much in antiquity – from other dynasties, the Welsh Tudors, for example, whose first ruler, Henry VII, had ascended the throne of England in 1485.

TOWARDS THE NATIONAL STATE

Only in England, France and Spain could there be discerned any real national cohesion and sentiment to sustain political unity. England, a relatively unimportant power, was a well-developed example. Insular, secluded from invasion and rid, after 1492, of continental appendages other than the seaports of Calais (finally lost only in 1558), her government was unusually centralized. The Tudors, anxious to assert the unity of the kingdom after the long period of disorder labelled the "Wars of the Roses", consciously associated national interest with that of the dynasty. Shakespeare quite naturally uses the language of patriotism (and, it may be remarked, says little about religious differences). France, too, had already come far along the road to national cohesion. The house of Valois-Bourbon had greater problems than the Tudors, though, in the continued survival of immunities and privileged enclaves within its territories over which its monarchs did not exercise full sovereignty as kings of France. Some of their subjects did not even speak French. Nevertheless, France was well on the way to becoming a national state.

This miniature portrays Ferdinand I of Habsburg (1503–1564) and is taken from his Book of Hours. Already First Regent of the patrimonial states of the House of Habsburg (the Austrian Archduchies), Ferdinand was named King of the Romans in 1531. He became Holy Roman Emperor in 1558.

HABSBURG PRE-EMINENCE

SPAIN WAS ALSO becoming a national state, though its two crowns were not united until the grandson of the Catholic Monarchs, Charles of Habsburg, became co-ruler with his insane mother in 1516 as Charles I. He had still carefully to distinguish the rights of Castile from those of Aragon, but Spanish nationality was made more self-conscious during his reign because, although at first popular, Charles obscured the national identity of Spain in a larger Habsburg empire and, indeed, sacrificed Spanish interest to dynastic aims and triumphs. The great diplomatic event of the first half of the century was his election in 1519 as Charles V, Holy Roman Emperor. He succeeded his grandfather Maximilian, who had sought his election, and careful marriages in the past had by then already made him the ruler of the furthest-flung territorial empire the world had ever

Charles I of Spain and V of Germany (1500–1558) is shown here in a portrait by Titian.

seen, to which the imperial title supplied a fitting crown. From his mother he inherited the Spanish kingdoms, the newly discovered Americas and Sicily. From his father, Maximilian's son, came the Netherlands which had been part of the duchy of Burgundy, and from his grandfather the Habsburg lands of Austria and the Tyrol, with Franche-Comté, Alsace and a bundle of claims in Italy. This was the greatest dynastic accumulation of the age, and the crowns of Bohemia and Hungary were held by Charles' brother, Ferdinand, who was to succeed him as emperor. Habsburg pre-eminence was the central fact of European politics for most of the sixteenth century. Its real and unreal pretensions are well shown in the list of Charles' titles when he ascended the imperial throne: "King of the Romans; Emperor-elect; semper Augustus; King of Spain, Sicily, Jerusalem, the Balearic Islands, the Canary Islands, the Indies and the mainland on the far side of the Atlantic; Archduke of Austria; Duke of Burgundy, Brabant, Styria, Carinthia, Carniola, Luxemburg, Limburg, Athens and Patras; Count of Habsburg, Flanders and Tyrol; Count Palatine of Burgundy, Hainault, Pfirt, Roussillon; Landgrave of Alsace; Count of Swabia; Lord of Asia and Africa."

THE IMPERIAL AMBITIONS OF CHARLES I

Whatever the conglomeration ruled by Charles I was, it was not national. It fell, for practical purposes, into two main blocks: the Spanish inheritance, rich through the possession of the Netherlands and irrigated by a growing flow of bullion from the Americas, and the old Habsburg lands, demanding an active role in Germany to maintain the family's pre-eminence there. Charles, though, saw from his imperial throne much more than this. Revealingly, he liked to call himself "God's standard-bearer" and campaigned like a Christian paladin of old against the Turk in Africa and up and down the Mediterranean. In his own eyes he was still the medieval emperor, much more than one ruler among many; he was leader of

Christendom and responsible only to God for his charge. Certainly he had a far better claim to be called "Defender of the Faith" than his Tudor rival Henry VIII, another aspirant to the imperial throne. Germany, Spain and Habsburg dynastic interest were all to be sacrificed in some degree to Charles' vision of his role. Yet what he sought was impossible. The dream of making a reality of universal empire was beyond the powers of any man given the strains imposed by the Reformation and the inadequate apparatus of sixteenth-century communication and administration. Charles, moreover, strove to rule personally, travelling ceaselessly in pursuit of this futile aim and thereby, perhaps, he ensured also that no part of his empire (unless it was the Netherlands) felt identified with his house. His aspiration reveals the way in which the medieval world still lived on, but also his anachronism.

The Holy Roman Empire was, of course, distinct from the Habsburg family possessions. It, too, embodied the medieval past, but at its most worm-eaten and unreal. Germany, where most of it lay, was a chaos supposedly united under the emperor and his tenants-in-chief, the imperial Diet. Since the Golden Bull the seven electors were virtually sovereign in their territories. There were also a hundred princes and more than fifty imperial cities, all independent. Another three hundred or so minor statelets and imperial vassals completed the patchwork which was what was left of the early medieval empire. As the sixteenth century began, an attempt to reform this confusion and give Germany some measure of national unity failed; this suited the lesser princes and the cities. All that emerged were some new administrative institutions. Charles' election as emperor in 1519 was by no means a foregone conclusion; rightly, people feared that German interests in the huge Habsburg dominions might be overridden or neglected. Heavy bribery of the electors was needed before he prevailed over the king of France (the only other serious candidate, for nobody believed that Henry VIII would be able to pay enough). Habsburg dynastic interest was thereafter the only unifying principle at work in the Holy Roman Empire until its abolition in 1806.

THE "ITALIAN" WARS

Italy, one of the most striking geographical unities in Europe, was also still fragmented into independent states, most of them ruled

Francis I of France (1494–1547), shown here in a portrait attributed to the French painter Jean Clouet (c.1485–c.1541), was Charles V's opponent in disputes over the control of territories including Burgundy, Milan, Genoa and Naples. Both were warring monarchs who fought personally in battle.

Emperor Charles V is shown entering the conquered city of Tunis in this 16th-century engraving. With its expansion from the western Mediterranean to the African Barbary Coast, however, the Turkish Empire also threatened Italy. Charles' conquest of Tunis in 1535 brought a brief halt to attacks by Barbary pirates supported by the Turks.

by princely despots, and some of them dependencies of external powers. The pope was a temporal monarch in the states of the Church. A king of Naples of the house of Aragon ruled that country. Sicily belonged to his Spanish relatives. Venice, Genoa and Lucca were republics. Milan was a large duchy of the Po valley ruled by the Sforza family. Florence was theoretically a republic but from 1509 really a monarchy in the hands of the Medici, a former banking house. In north Italy the dukes of Savoy ruled Piedmont, on the other side of the Alps from

their own ancestral lands. The divisions of the peninsula made it an attractive prey and a tangle of family relationships gave French and Spanish rulers excuses to dabble in affairs there. For the first half of the sixteenth century the main theme of European diplomatic history is provided by the rivalry of Habsburg and Bourbon, and its main theatre and its prizes lay in Italy.

A series of Habsburg-Valois wars in Italy began in 1494 with a French invasion reminiscent of medieval adventuring and raiding, and lasted until 1559. They constitute a distinct period in the evolution of the European states system. Charles V's accession and the defeat of Francis in the imperial election brought out the lines of dynastic competition more clearly. There were altogether six "Italian" wars and they were more important than they might at first appear. To Charles the Emperor, they were a fatal distraction from the Reformation problem, and to Charles the King of Spain they were the start of a fatal draining of their country's power. To the French, they brought impoverishment and invasion, and to their kings, in the end, frustration, for Spain was left dominant in Italy. To the inhabitants of that country, the wars brought a variety of disasters. For the first time since the age of the barbarian invasions, Rome was sacked (in 1527, by a mutinous imperial army) and Spanish hegemony finally ended the great days of the city republics and brought about the emigration of skilled craftsmen. At one time, the coasts of Italy were raided by French and Turkish ships in concert; the hollowness of the unity of Christendom was revealed by a formal alliance of a French king with the Sultan.

Perhaps these were good years only for the Ottomans. Venice, usually left to face the Turks alone, watched her empire in the eastern Mediterranean begin to crumble away. Both Charles V and his son were defeated in

African enterprises and the defeat of the Turks at Lepanto in 1571 was only a momentary setback for them; three years later they took back Tunis from the Spanish. The struggle with the Ottomans and the support of the Habsburg cause in Italy had by then overburdened even Spain's flow of silver from America, a recourse badly needed by her at home. In his last years, Charles V was crippled by debt.

THE ABDICATION OF CHARLES

Charles V abdicated in 1556, just after the first settlement at Augsburg of the religious disputes of Germany, to be succeeded as emperor by his brother, who took the Austrian inheritance, and as ruler of Spain by his son, Philip II, a Spaniard born and bred. Charles had been born in the Netherlands and the ceremony which ended the great emperor's reign took place there, in the Hall of the Golden Fleece; he was moved to tears as he left the assembly, leaning on the shoulder of a young nobleman, William of Orange. This division of the Habsburg inheritance marks the watershed of European affairs in the 1550s.

What followed was the blackest period of Europe's history for centuries. With a brief lull as it opened, European rulers and their people indulged in the seventeenth century in an orgy of hatred, bigotry, massacre, torture and brutality which has no parallel until the twentieth. The dominating facts of this period were the military pre-eminence of Spain, the ideological conflict opened by the Counter-Reformation, the paralysis of Germany and, for a long time, France, by internal religious quarrels, the emergence of new centres of power in England, the Dutch Netherlands and Sweden, and the first adumbrations of the overseas conflicts of the next two

centuries. Only with the end of this period did it appear that the power of Spain had dwindled and that France had inherited her continental ascendancy.

THE DUTCH REVOLT

The best starting-point in an assessment of seventeenth-century Europe is the Dutch Revolt. Like the Spanish Civil War of 1936–9 (but for much longer) it mixed up the relations of many outsiders in a confusion of ideological, political, strategic and economic issues. France could not be easy while Spanish

Philip II of Spain (1527–1598), the son of Charles I, was known as "Defender of the Faith". However, Philip, like his father, did not hesitate to enter into conflict with the papacy, for which he was excommunicated.

armies might invade her from Spain, Italy and Flanders. England's involvement arose in other ways. Though she was Protestant, she was only just Protestant, and Philip tried to avoid an outright break with Elizabeth I. He was for a long time unwilling to sacrifice the chance of reasserting the English interests he had won by marriage to Mary Tudor, and thought he might retain them by marrying a second English queen. Moreover he was long distracted by campaigns against the Ottomans. But national and religious feeling were inflamed in England by Spanish responses to English piracy at the expense of the Spanish empire; Anglo-Spanish relations decayed rapidly in the 1570s and 1580s. Elizabeth overtly and covertly helped the Dutch, whom she did not want to see go under, but did so without enthusiasm; being a monarch, she did not like rebels. In the end, armed with papal approval for the deposition

of Elizabeth, the heretic queen, a great Spanish invasion effort was mounted in 1588. "God blew and they were scattered" said the inscription on an English commemorative medal; bad weather completed the work of Spanish planning and English seamanship and gunnery (though not a ship on either side was sunk by gunfire) to bring the Armada to disaster. War with Spain went on long after its shattered remnants had limped back to Spanish harbours but a great danger was over. Also, almost incidentally, an English naval tradition of enormous importance had been born.

THE THIRTY YEARS' WAR

James I strove sensibly to avoid a renewal of the conflict once peace had been made and succeeded, for all the anti-Spanish prejudices

The Congress of Münster of 15 May 1648, a scene from which is depicted in this 17th-century painting, was one of two parallel conferences that marked the start of the European peace process to end the Thirty Years' War. The conference in Münster was attended by representatives of the Catholic powers, while the envoys from the Protestant states met in Osnabrück.

France and Spain continued fighting after the signing of the Peace of Westphalia (1648). Hostilities between them did not end until 1659, by which time French predominance in western Europe was firmly established. In this engraving, Louis XIV of France and Navarre and Philip IV of Spain meet in 1659 to ratify the Peace of the Pyrenees, which put an end the fighting.

of his subjects. England was not sucked into the continental conflict when the revolt of the Netherlands, re-ignited after a Twelve Years' Truce, was merged into a much greater struggle, the Thirty Years' War. Its heart was a Habsburg attempt to rebuild the imperial authority in Germany by linking it with the triumph of the Counter-Reformation. This called in question the Peace of Augsburg and the survival of a religiously pluralistic Germany. Once again, cross-currents confused the pattern of ideological conflict. As Habsburg and Valois had disputed Italy in the sixteenth century, Habsburg and Bourbon disputed Germany in the next. Dynastic interest brought Catholic France into the field against the Catholic Habsburgs. Under the leadership of a cardinal, the "eldest daughter of the Church", as France was claimed to be, allied with Dutch Calvinists and Swedish Lutherans to assure the rights of German princes. Meanwhile the unhappy inhabitants of much of central Europe had often to endure the whims and rapacities of quasi-

independent warlords. Cardinal Richelieu has a better claim than any other man to be the creator of a foreign policy of stirring up trouble beyond the Rhine which was to serve France well for over a century. If anyone still doubted it, with him the age of *Realpolitik* and *raison d'état*, of simple, unprincipled assertion of the interest of the sovereign state, had clearly arrived.

The Peace of Westphalia which ended the Thirty Years' War in 1648 was in several ways a registration of change. Yet it showed traces still of the fading past. This makes it a good vantage-point. It was the end of the era of religious wars in Europe; for the last time European statesmen had as one of their main concerns in a general settlement the religious future of their peoples. It also marked the end of Spanish military supremacy and of the dream of reconstituting the empire of Charles V. It closed, too, an era of Habsburg history. In Germany a new force had appeared in the Electorate of Brandenburg, with which later Habsburgs would contend,

Europe at the time of the Treaty of Westphalia, 1648

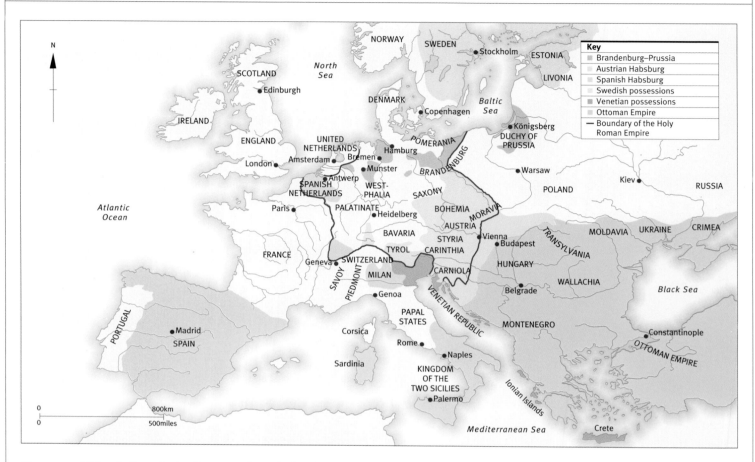

The peace of Westphalia undoubtedly meant the end of Habsburg domination in Europe and particularly of its Spanish branch. However, although a "European balance" was now spoken of for the first time, new great powers emerged after the treaties: France and Sweden. At first, a policy of religious tolerance was introduced; the empire was divided into a confederation of independent states where the individual princes' power was much greater than that of the emperor. But these treaties did not bring about general peace in Europe, since the Baltic problems remained unresolved and the war between France and Spain continued.

but the frustration of Habsburg aims in Germany had been the work of outsiders, Sweden and France. Here was the real sign of the future: a period of French ascendancy was beginning in Europe west of the Elbe.

THE RISE OF COLONIAL INTEREST

A century and a half after Columbus, when Spain, Portugal, England, France and Holland all already had important overseas empires, these were apparently of no interest to the authors of the peace. England was not even represented at either of the centres of negotiation; she had hardly been concerned in what was at issue once the first phase of the war was over. Preoccupied by internal quarrels and troubled by her Scots neighbours, her foreign policy was directed towards ends more extra-European than European – though it was these ends which soon led her to fight the Dutch (1552–4). Although Cromwell quickly restored peace, telling the

The port of Rotterdam near Delft, in Holland, is shown in this engraving. Rotterdam was one of Holland's thriving commercial ports during the 16th and 17th centuries.

Dutch there was room in the world for both of them to trade, English and Dutch diplomacy was already showing more clearly than that of other nations the influence of commercial and colonial interest.

THE FRANCE OF LOUIS XIV

FRENCH ASCENDANCY was founded on solid natural advantages. France was the most populous state of western Europe and on this simple fact rested French military power until the nineteenth century; it would always require the assembling of great international forces to contain it. France, however miserably poor its inhabitants may seem to modern eyes, had great economic resources, and was able to sustain a huge efflorescence of power and prestige under Louis XIV. His reign began formally in 1643, but actually in 1661 when, at the age of twenty-two, he announced his intention of managing his own affairs. This assumption of supreme power was a great fact in international as well as French history; Louis was the most consummate exponent of the trade of kingship who has ever lived. Only for convenience may his foreign policy be distinguished from other aspects of his reign. The building of Versailles, for example, was not only the gratification of a personal taste, but an exercise in building a prestige essential to his diplomacy. Similarly, though they may be separated, his foreign and domestic policy were closely entwined with one another and with ideology. Louis might wish to improve the strategical shape of France's northwestern frontier, but also (though he might buy millions of tulip bulbs a year from them for Versailles) he despised the Dutch as merchants, disapproved of them as republicans, and detested them as Protestants. Nor was that all. Louis was a legalistic man – kings had to be – and

The Palace of Versailles is depicted in this 18th-century engraving. Louis XIV (the "Sun King") intended the palace to glorify the French monarchy, which meant that art of every kind was collected on an unrestrained scale. The court of the Sun King and the salons of Paris were copied throughout Europe. In Germany, Poland and Russia such imitation went so far as the adoption of French as the second, or even the first, language of educated society.

he felt easier when there existed legal claims good enough to give respectability to what he was doing. This was the complicated background to a foreign policy of expansion. Though in the end it cost his country dearly, it carried France to a pre-eminence from which she was to freewheel through half the eighteenth century, and created a legend to which the French still look back with nostalgia.

FRENCH AGGRESSION

Louis' first aim was an improved frontier. This meant conflict with Spain, still in possession of the Spanish Netherlands and the Franche-Comté. The defeat of Spain opened the way to war with the Dutch. The Dutch held their own, but the war ended in 1678 with a peace usually reckoned the peak of Louis' achievement in foreign affairs. He now turned to Germany. Besides territorial conquest, he sought the imperial crown and to obtain it was willing to ally with the Turk. A turning-point came in 1688, when William of Orange, the stadtholder of Holland, took his wife Mary Stuart to England to replace her father on the English throne. From this time Louis had a new and persistent enemy across the Channel, instead of the complaisant Stuart kings. Dutch William could deploy the resources of the leading Protestant country and for the first time since the days of Cromwell, England fielded an army on the continent in support of a league of European states (even the pope joined it secretly) against Louis. King William's war (or the war of the League of Augsburg), brought together Spain and Austria, as well as the Protestant states of Europe, to contain the overweening ambition of the French king. The peace which ended it was the first in which he had to make concessions.

THE WAR OF THE SPANISH SUCCESSION

In 1700 Charles II of Spain died childless. It was an event Europe had long awaited, for he had been a sickly, feeble-minded fellow. Enormous diplomatic preparations had been made for his demise because of the great danger and opportunity which it must present. A huge dynastic inheritance was at stake. A tangle of claims arising from marriage alliances in the past meant that the Habsburg emperor and Louis XIV (who had passed his rights in the matter on to his grandson) would have to dispute the matter. But everyone was interested. The English wanted to know what would happen to the trade of Spanish America, the Dutch the fate of the Spanish Netherlands. The prospect of an undivided inheritance going either to Bourbon or Habsburg alarmed everybody. The ghost of Charles V's empire walked again. Partition treaties had therefore been made. But Charles II's will left the whole Spanish inheritance to Louis' grandson. Louis accepted it, setting aside the agreements into which he had entered. He also offended the English by recognizing the exiled Stuart Pretender as James III of England. A Grand Alliance of emperor, United Provinces and England was soon formed, and there began the War of the Spanish Succession, twelve years' fighting, which eventually drove Louis to terms. By treaties signed in 1713 and 1714 and called the Peace of Utrecht, the crowns of Spain and

France were declared for ever incapable of being united. The first Bourbon king of Spain took his place on the Spanish throne, though, taking with Spain the Indies but not the Netherlands, which went to the emperor as compensation and to provide a tripwire defence for the Dutch against further French aggression. Austria also profited in Italy. France made concessions overseas to Great Britain (as it was after the union of England with Scotland in 1707). The Stuart Pretender was expelled from France and Louis recognized the Protestant succession in England.

The king of Spain is depicted attending mass in this painting entitled *Adoration of the Sacred Host by Charles II*.

The Battle of Almansa in southeast Spain, depicted here, was a turning point mid-way through the War of the Spanish Succession. A Bourbon victory on April 24, 1707, consolidated Philip V's reign as King of Spain. But French reverses elsewhere soon ensured that Philip would not retain all Spain's possessions nor ever combine the thrones of Spain and France.

THE STABILIZATION OF WESTERN POLITICAL BOUNDARIES

The terms of the Peace of Utrecht assured the virtual stabilization of western continental Europe until the French Revolution seventy-five years later. Not everyone liked it (the emperor refused to admit the end of his claim to the throne of Spain) but to a remarkable degree the major definitions of western Europe north of the Alps have remained what they were in 1714. Belgium, of course, did not exist, but the Austrian Netherlands occupied much of the same area as that country, and the United Provinces corresponds to the modern Netherlands. France would keep Franche-Comté and, except between 1871 and 1918, the Alsace and Lorraine which Louis XIV had won for her. Spain and Portugal would after 1714 remain separate within their present boundaries; they still had large colonial empires but were never again to be able to deploy their potential strength so as to rise out of the second rank of powers.

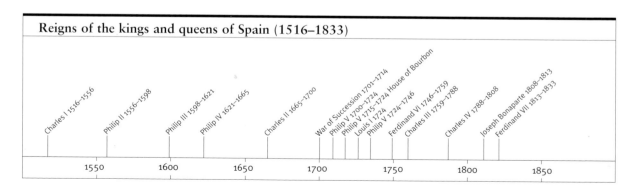

Reigns of the kings and queens of Spain (1516–1833)

Charles I 1516–1556
Philip II 1556–1598
Philip III 1598–1621
Philip IV 1621–1665
Charles II 1665–1700
War of Succession 1701–1714
Philip V 1700–1724 House of Bourbon
Philip V 1715–1724
Louis I 1724
Philip V 1724–1746
Ferdinand VI 1746–1759
Charles III 1759–1788
Charles IV 1788–1808
Joseph Bonaparte 1808–1813
Ferdinand VII 1813–1833

1550   1600   1650   1700   1750   1800   1850

Great Britain was the new great power in the West; since 1707, England no longer had to bother about the old northern threat, though once more attached by a personal connexion to the continent because after 1714 her rulers were also electors of Hanover. South of the Alps, the dust took longer to settle. A still disunited Italy underwent another thirty-odd years of uncertainty, minor representatives of European royal houses shuffling around it from one state to another in attempts to tie up the loose ends and seize the leftovers of the age of dynastic rivalry. After 1748 there was only one important native dynasty left in the peninsula, that of Savoy, which ruled Piedmont on the south side of the Alps and the island of Sardinia. The Papal States, it is true, could since the fifteenth century be regarded as an Italian monarchy, though only occasionally a dynastic one, and the decaying republics of Venice, Genoa and Lucca also upheld the tattered standard of Italian independence. Foreign rulers were installed in the other states.

THE AGE OF NATIONAL POLITICS

Western political geography was thus set for a long time. Immediately, this owed much to the need felt by all statesmen to avoid for as long as possible another conflict such as that which had just closed. For the first time a treaty of 1713 declared the aim of the signatories to be the security of peace through a balance of power. So practical an aim was an important innovation in political thinking. There were good grounds for such realism; wars were more expensive than ever and even Great Britain and France, the only countries in the eighteenth century capable of sustaining war against other great powers without foreign subsidy, had been strained. But the end of the War of the Spanish Succession also brought effective settlements of real problems. A new age was opening. Outside Italy, most of the political map of the twentieth century was already visible in western Europe. Dynasticism was beginning to be relegated to the second rank as a principle of

Under the long sultanate of Suleiman the Magnificent (1520–1566) the Turkish Empire managed to threaten Europe from the east by advancing towards the Balkans, occupying Hungary after the Battle of Mohács (1527) in which King Louis II died, and in 1529 closing in on Vienna for the first time. In 1532, it took all the efforts of the Holy Roman Emperor, Charles V, to end the siege of that city, as shown in this engraving.

foreign policy. The age of national politics had begun, for some monarchs, at least, who could no longer separate the interests of their house from those of their nation.

East of the Rhine (and still more east of the Elbe) none of this was true. Great changes had already occurred there and many more were to come before 1800. But their origins have to be traced back a long way, as far as the beginning of the sixteenth century. At that time Europe's eastern frontiers were guarded by Habsburg Austria and the vast Polish-Lithuanian kingdom ruled by the Jagiellons which had been formed by marriage in the fourteenth century. They shared with the maritime empire of Venice the burden of resistance to Ottoman power, the supreme fact of East European politics at that moment. The phrase "Eastern Question" had not then been invented; if it had been, its users would have meant by it the problem of defending Europe against Islam. The Turks won victories and made conquests as late as the eighteenth century, though by then their last

great effort was spent. For more than two centuries after the capture of Constantinople, nevertheless, they set the terms of Eastern European diplomacy and strategy.

THE OTTOMAN THREAT

THE CAPTURE of Constantinople was followed by more than a century of naval warfare and Turkish expansion to the west from which the main sufferer was Venice. While she long remained rich by comparison with other Italian states, Venice suffered a relative decline, first in military and then in commercial power. The first, which led to the second, was the result of a long, losing battle against the Turks. In 1479, they took the Ionian islands and imposed an annual charge for trade in the Black Sea. Though Venice acquired Cyprus two years later, and turned it into a major base, it was in its turn lost in 1571. By 1600, though still (thanks to her manufacturers) a rich state, Venice had lost her commercial leaderships; first Antwerp and then Amsterdam had replaced her. She was no longer a mercantile power at the level of the United Provinces or even England. Turkish success was interrupted in the early seventeenth century but then resumed; in 1669 the Venetians had to recognize that they had lost Crete. Meanwhile, Hungary was invaded in 1664. This was the last Turkish conquest of a European kingdom, though the Ukrainians soon acknowledged Turkish suzerainty and the Poles had to give up Podolia. In 1683 the Turks opened a siege of Vienna and Europe seemed in its greatest danger for over two centuries. In fact it was not. This was to be the last time Vienna was besieged, for the great days of Ottoman power were over. The effort which began with the conquest of Hungary had been the last heave.

Sultan Mehmet II ("the Conqueror") (1429–1481), is portrayed in this painting of 1480 by Gentile Bellini (c.1429–1507). Mehmet II established the capital of the Ottoman Empire in Istanbul, began the expansion towards the Balkans and attacked Venetian possessions.

OTTOMAN DECLINE

Difficulties had long troubled the Ottomans. Their army was no longer abreast of the latest military technology: it lacked the field artillery which had become the decisive weapon of the seventeenth-century battlefield. At sea, the Turks clung to the old galley tactics of ramming and boarding and were less and less successful against the Atlantic nations' technique of using the ship as a floating artillery battery (unfortunately for themselves, the Venetians were conservative too). Turkish power was in any case badly overstretched. It was pinned down in Asia (where the conquest of Iraq from Persia in 1639 brought almost the whole Arab-Islamic world under Ottoman rule) as well as in Europe and Africa, and the strain was too much for a structure allowed to relax by inadequate or incompetent rulers. A great vizier had pulled things together in the middle of the century to make the last offensives possible. But there were weaknesses which he could not correct, for they were inherent in the nature of the empire itself.

More a military occupation than a political unity, Ottoman empire was dangerously dependent on subjects whose loyalty it could not win. The Ottomans usually respected the customs and institutions of non-Muslim communities, which were ruled under the *millet* system, through their own authorities. The Greek Orthodox, Armenians and Jews were the most important and each had their own arrangements, the Greek Christians having to pay a special poll-tax, for example, and being ruled, ultimately, by their own patriarch in Constantinople. At lower levels, such arrangements as seemed best were made with leaders of local communities for the support of the military machine which was the heart of the Ottoman structure. In the end this bred over-mighty subjects as pashas feathered their own nests amid incoherence and inefficiency. It gave the subjects of the sultan no sense of identification with his rule but, rather, alienated them from it while the Ottoman lands in Europe grew poorer.

THE OTTOMAN RETREAT IN EUROPE

The year 1683, although a good symbolic date as the last time that Europe stood upon

The Ottoman sultan Selim I (1467–1520), shown in this manuscript illustration on a sailing outing, conquered Syria, Arabia and Egypt and ordered the Turkish siege of Vienna.

Sultan Mustafa II, son of Mehmet IV, ruled the Ottoman Empire from 1695 to 1703. His reign was plagued by confrontations with the members of the Holy League (Austria, Venice, Poland and Russia), with whom he signed the Peace of Karlowitz in 1699. From that time, the power of the Ottoman Empire began to diminish.

the defensive in her old bastion against Islam before going over to the attack, was a less dangerous moment than it looked. Afterwards the tide of Turkish power was to ebb almost without interruption until in 1918 it was once more confined to the immediate hinterland of Constantinople and the old Ottoman heartland, Anatolia. The relief of Vienna by the king of Poland, John Sobieski, was followed by the liberation of Hungary. The dethronement of an unsuccessful sultan in 1687 and his incarceration in a cage proved no cure for Turkish weakness. In 1699 Hungary became part of the Habsburg dominions again, devastated though it was. In the following century Transylvania, the Bukovina, and most of the Black Sea coasts would follow it out of Ottoman control. By 1800, the Russians had asserted a special protection over the Christian subjects of the Ottomans and had already tried promoting

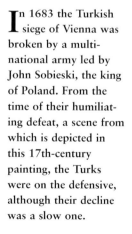

In 1683 the Turkish siege of Vienna was broken by a multinational army led by John Sobieski, the king of Poland. From the time of their humiliating defeat, a scene from which is depicted in this 17th-century painting, the Turks were on the defensive, although their decline was a slow one.

rebellion among them. In the eighteenth century, too, Ottoman rule ebbed in Africa and Asia; by the end of it, though forms might be preserved, the Ottoman caliphate was somewhat like that of the Abbasids in their declining days. Morocco, Algeria, Tunis, Egypt, Syria, Mesopotamia and Arabia were all in varying degrees independent or semi-independent.

POLAND

IT WAS NOT THE TRADITIONAL GUARDIANS of eastern Europe, the once-great Polish-Lithuanian commonwealth and the Habsburgs, who were the legatees of the Ottoman heritage, nor they who inflicted the most punishing blows as the Ottoman Empire crumbled. The Poles were in fact nearing the

The beginning of the Ottoman retreat in Europe

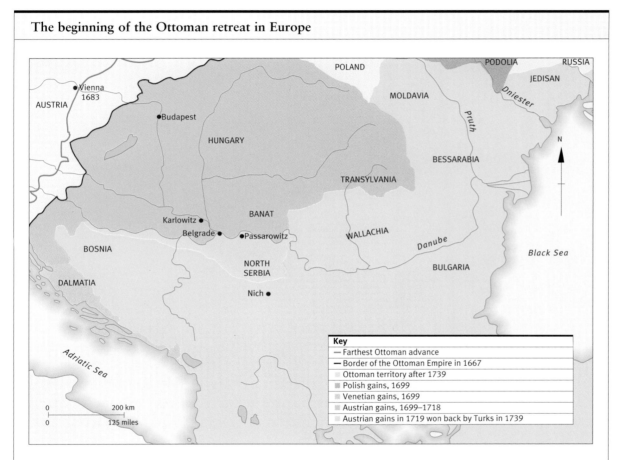

Key
— Farthest Ottoman advance
— Border of the Ottoman Empire in 1667
▢ Ottoman territory after 1739
▨ Polish gains, 1699
▨ Venetian gains, 1699
▨ Austrian gains, 1699–1718
▢ Austrian gains in 1719 won back by Turks in 1739

By the middle of the 16th century, the Turkish Empire practically equalled Justinian's Byzantine Empire in size, and was governed from a resplendent Istanbul. The great pillars of the Ottoman Empire were a well-disciplined, highly skilled army, access to plentiful human and natural resources and a stable leadership provided by the dynastic and governmental institutions. However, when expansion ground to a halt and then went into reverse in the 18th century, these pillars disintegrated – a process accompanied by misery and oppression. The Ottoman Empire became

a target for the European monarchies. The Treaty of Karlowitz, signed in 1699, ended the "Vienna War" and forced the Ottomans to concede land to Poland, Austria and Venice. At Passarowitz in 1718 a treaty was signed giving the Habsburg emperor more Ottoman territories, although Austria was forced to return some land to the Ottoman Empire by the Treaty of Belgrade in 1739. Only the rivalries between the various European powers allowed the Ottoman Empire, which was almost incapable of defending itself by 1800, to survive until the 19th century.

Queen Christina of Sweden (1626–1689), who is depicted with her court in this 17th-century painting, ended Sweden's military expansion into Europe during the Thirty Years' War at the Peace of Westphalia in 1648.

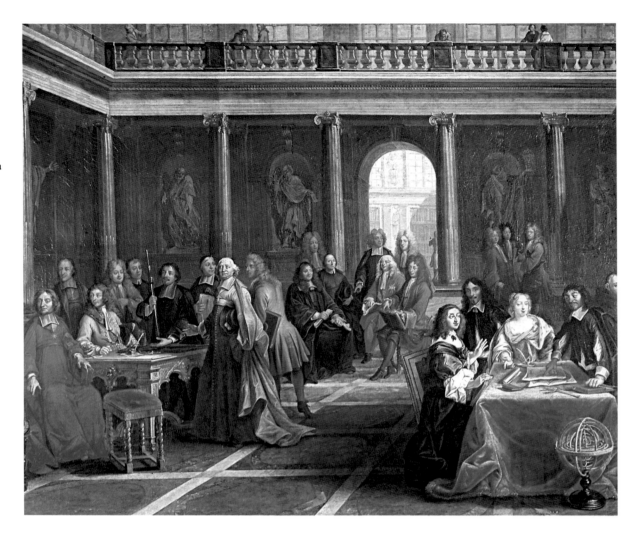

end of their own history as an independent nation. The personal union of Lithuania and Poland had been turned into a real union of the two countries too late. In 1572, when the last king of the Jagiellon line died without an heir, the throne had become not only theoretically but actually elective. His successor was French and for the next century Polish magnates and foreign kings disputed each election, while their country was under grave and continuing pressure from Turks, Russians and Swedes. Poland prospered against these enemies only when they were embarrassed elsewhere. The Swedes descended on her northern territories during the Thirty Years' War and the last of the Polish coast was given up to them in 1660. Internal divisions

had worsened, too; the Counter-Reformation brought religious persecution to the Polish Protestants and there were risings of Cossacks in the Ukraine and continuing serf revolts.

THE POLISH SOCIAL STRUCTURE

The election as king of the heroic John Sobieski was the last which was not the outcome of machinations by foreign rulers. He had won important victories and managed to preside over Poland's curious and highly decentralized constitution. The elected kings had very little legal power to balance that of the landowners. They had no standing army and could rely only on their own personal troops when factions among the gentry or magnates fell back on the practice of armed rebellion ("Confederation") to obtain their wishes. In the Diet, the central parliamentary body of the kingdom, a rule of unanimity stood in the way of any reform. Yet reform was badly needed, if a geographically ill-defined, religiously divided Poland, ruled by a narrowly selfish rural gentry, was to survive. Poland was a medieval community in a modernizing world.

John Sobieski could do nothing to change this. Poland's social structure was strongly resistant to reform. The nobility or gentry were effectively the clients of a few great families of extraordinary wealth. One clan, the Radziwills, owned estates half the size of Ireland and held a court which outshone that of Warsaw; the Potocki estates covered 6,500 square miles (roughly half the area of the Dutch Republic). The smaller landowners could not stand up to such grandees. Their estates made up less than a tenth of Poland in 1700. The million or so gentry who were legally the Polish "nation" were for the most

part poor, and therefore dominated by great magnates reluctant to surrender their power to arrange a confederation or manipulate a Diet. At the bottom of the pile were the peasants, some of the most miserable in Europe, engaged in unending battle with their landlords over feudal dues, over whom landlords still had in 1700 rights of life and death. The towns were powerless. Their total population was only half the size of the gentry and they had been devastated by the seventeenth-century wars. Yet Prussia and Russia also rested on backward agrarian and feudal infrastructures and survived. Poland was the only one of the three eastern states to go under completely. The principle of election blocked the emergence of Polish Tudors or Bourbons who could identify their own dynastic instincts of self-aggrandizement with those of the nation. Poland entered the eighteenth century under a foreign king, the

This painting is one of a series of 24 views of Warsaw painted by the Italian artist Bernardo Bellotto, who resided in the Polish capital from 1767 until his death in 1780.

John III of Poland (1624–1696), known as John Sobieski, is portrayed in this 17th-century painting. A distinguished soldier, he was elected king of Poland in 1674. When Poland, Saxony, Bavaria and many other small German principalities sent troops to defend Vienna against the Turks in 1683, John Sobieski led the army to victory, thereby becoming a hero of Christian Europe.

The suspicious watchfulness of the Russian tsar Ivan IV (1530–1584), who is depicted in this icon portrait, affected not only state structures, but also the Russian Orthodox Church, to which he introduced the Orthodox calendar and canonical law. Ivan "the Terrible" is also remembered for the brutal way in which he persecuted, murdered or deported thousands of boyars.

Elector of Saxony, who was chosen to succeed John Sobieski in 1697, soon deposed by the Swedes, and then put back again on his throne by the Russians.

RUSSIAN POWER AND IVAN THE TERRIBLE

RUSSIA WAS THE COMING new great power in the East. Her national identity had been barely discernible in 1500. Two hundred years later her potential was still only beginning to dawn on most Western statesmen, though the Poles and Swedes were already alive to it. It now requires an effort to realize how rapid and astonishing was the appearance as a major force of what was to become one of the two most powerful states in the world. At the beginning of the European age, when only the ground-plan of the Russian future had been laid out by Ivan the Great, such an outcome was inconceivable, and so it long remained. The first man formally to bear the title of "Tsar of all the Russias" was his grandson Ivan IV, crowned in 1547; and the conferment of the title at his coronation was meant to say that the Grand Prince of Muscovy had become an emperor ruling many peoples. In spite of a ferocious vigour which earned him his nickname "the Terrible", he played no significant role in European affairs. So little was Russia known even in the next century that a French king could write to a tsar, not knowing that the prince whom he addressed had been dead for ten years. The shape of a future Russia was slowly determined, and almost unnoticed in the West. Even after Ivan the Great, Russia had remained territorially ill-defined and exposed. The Turks had pushed into southeast Europe. Between them and Muscovy lay the Ukraine, the lands of the Cossacks, peoples who fiercely protected their independence. So long as they had no powerful neighbours, they found it easy to do so. To the east of Russia, the Urals provided a theoretical though hardly a realistic frontier. Russia's rulers have always found it easy to feel isolated in the middle of hostile space. Almost instinctively, they have sought natural frontiers at its edges or a protective glacis of clients.

The first steps had to be the consolidation of the gains of Ivan the Great which constituted the Russian heartland. Then came penetration of the wilderness of the north. When Ivan the Terrible came to the throne, Russia had a small Baltic coast and a vast territory stretching up to the White Sea, thinly inhabited by scattered and primitive peoples, but providing a route to the west; in 1584 the port of Archangel was founded.

The Cathedral of St Basil the Blessed was built between 1554 and 1560 outside the Kremlin in Moscow, following Ivan IV's victory over the Tatars (Mongols) of Kazan and Astrakhan.

Ivan could do little on the Baltic front but successfully turned on the Tatars after they burned Moscow yet again in 1571. He drove them from Kazan and Astrakhan and won control of the whole length of the Volga, carrying Muscovite power as far as the Caspian Sea.

ASIAN EXPANSION UNDER IVAN

The other great thrust which began in his reign was across the Urals, into Siberia, and was to be less one of conquest than of settlement. Even today, most of the Russian republic is in Asia, and for nearly two centuries a world as

During the reign of Ivan III, known as Ivan the Great, Moscow (seen here in a 16th-century illustration) was a commercial centre that exported cereals, linen and fodder. The creation of the English Muscovy Company later brought the city increasingly under Western influence. In the 17th century, numerous European merchants lived in a special district called the Sloboda.

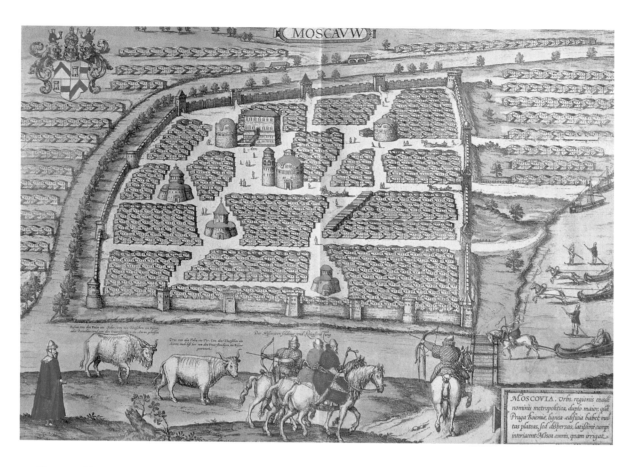

well as a European power was ruled by the tsars and their successors. The first steps towards this outcome were an ironic anticipation of what was to be a theme of the major Siberian frontier in later times: the first Russian settlers across the Urals seem to have been political refugees from Novgorod. Among those who followed were others fleeing from serfdom (there were no serfs in Siberia) and aggrieved Cossacks. By 1600 there were Russian settlements as much as six hundred miles beyond the Urals, closely supervised by a competent bureaucracy out to assure the state tribute in furs. The rivers were the keys to the region, more important even than those of the American frontier. Within fifty years a man and his goods could travel by river with only three portages from Tobolsk, three hundred miles east of the Urals, to the port of Okhotsk, three thousand miles away. There he would be only four hundred miles by sea from Sakhalin, the northernmost of the major islands of the chain which makes up Japan – a sea-passage about as long as that from Land's End to Antwerp. By 1700 there were 200,000 settlers east of the Urals: it had by then been possible already to agree the treaty of Nerchinsk with the Chinese and some Russians, we are told, talked of the conquest of China.

RUSSIA AND THE WEST

The movement eastward was not much affected by the upheavals and dangers of the "Time of Troubles" which followed Ivan's death, though in the west there were moments when the outlet to the Baltic was lost and when even Moscow and Novgorod were occupied by Lithuanians or Poles. Russia was still not a serious European power in the early seventeenth century. The then rising strength of Sweden was thrown against her and it was not until the great war of 1654–67 that the tsars finally regained Smolensk and Little Russia, not to be lost again (and then only briefly) until 1812. Maps and treaties now began to define Russia in the west in a way which had some reality. By 1700, though she still had no Black Sea coast, her southwestern frontier ran on the western side of the Dnieper for most of its length, embracing the great historic city of Kiev and the Cossacks who lived on the east bank. They had appealed to the tsar for protection from the Poles and were granted special, semi-autonomous governmental arrangements which survived until Soviet times. Most Russian gains had been at the expense of Poland, long preoccupied with fighting off Turk and Swede. But Russian armies joined the Poles in alliance against the Ottomans in 1687; this was a historic moment, too, for it was the beginning of the classical Eastern Question which was to trouble European statesmen until 1918, when they found that the problem of deciding what limit, if any, should be placed upon Russian encroachment on the Ottoman Empire had at last disappeared with the protagonists themselves.

The making of Russia was overwhelmingly a political act. The monarchy was its centre and motor; the country had no racial unity to pre-ordain its existence and precious little geographical definition to impose a shape. If it was united by Orthodoxy, other Slavs were Orthodox, too. The growth of the personal domain and power of the tsars was the key to the building of the nation. Ivan the Terrible was an administrative reformer. Under him appeared the beginnings of a nobility owing military service in return for their estates, a development of a system employed by the princes of Muscovy to obtain levies to fight the Tatars. It made possible the raising of an army which led the king of Poland to warn the English queen, Elizabeth I, that if they got hold of Western technical skills the Russians would be unbeatable; the danger was remote, but this was prescient.

THE ROMANOVS AND THE TAMING OF THE CHURCH

From time to time Russia suffered setbacks, though the survival of the state does not seem in retrospect to have been at stake. The last tsar of the house of Rurik died in 1598. Usurpation and the disputing of the throne between noble families and Polish interventionists went on until 1613, when the first tsar of a new house, Michael Romanov, emerged. Though a weak ruler who lived in the shadow of his dominating father, he founded a dynasty which was to rule Russia for three hundred years, until the tsarist state

The boyars, wealthy landowners, constituted Russia's upper nobility. The picture shows a group of boyars who were sent to the court of the Holy Roman Emperor Maximilian II in 1576. They are bearing gifts from Russia for the emperor, including furs.

itself collapsed. His immediate successors fought off rival nobles and humbled the great ones among them, the boyars, who had attempted to revive a power curbed by Ivan the Terrible. Beyond their ranks the only potential internal rival was the Church. In the seventeenth century it was weakened by schism and in 1667 a great step in Russian history was taken when the patriarch was deprived after a quarrel with the tsar. There was to be no Investiture Contest in Russia. After this time the Russian Church was structurally and legally subordinated to a lay official. Among believers there would emerge plenty of spontaneous doctrinal and moral opposition to current Orthodoxy, and there began the long-lived and culturally very important movement of underground religious dissent called the *raskol* which would eventually feed political opposition. But Russia was never to know the conflict of Church and State which was so creative a force in Western Europe, any more than she was to know the stimulus of the Reformation.

TSARIST AUTOCRACY

The outcome of the subordination of the Russian Church to royal authority was the final evolution of the enduring Russian governmental form, tsarist autocracy. It was characterized by the personification in the ruler of a semi-sacrosanct authority unlimited by clear legal checks, by an emphasis on the service owed to him by all subjects, by the linking of landholding to this idea, by the idea that all institutions within the state except the Church derived from it and had no independent standing of their own, by the lack of a distinction of powers and the development of a huge bureaucracy, and by the paramountcy of military needs. These qualities, as the scholar who listed them pointed out, were not

all present at the start, nor were all of them equally operative and obvious at all times. But they mark tsardom off from monarchy in Western Christendom where, far back in the Middle Ages, towns, estates of the realm, guilds and many other bodies had established the privileges and liberties on which later constitutionalism was to be built. In old Muscovy, the highest official had a title which meant "slave" or "servant" at a time when, in neighbouring Poland-Lithuania, his opposite number was designated "citizen". Even Louis XIV, though he might believe in Divine Right and aspire to unrivalled power, always conceived it to be a power explicitly restricted by rights, by religion, by divinely ordained law. Though his subjects knew he was an absolute monarch, they were sure he was not a despot. In England an even more startlingly different monarchy was developing, one under the control of Parliament. Divergent from one another though English and French monarchical practice might be, they both accepted practical and theoretical limitations inconceivable to tsardom; they bore the stamp of a Western tradition Russia had never known. For the whole of its existence the Russian autocracy was to be in the West a byword for despotism.

Yet it suited Russia. Moreover, the attitudes which underlay it seem in some measure to suit Russia still. Eighteenth-century sociologists used to suggest that big, flat countries favoured despotism. This was over-simple, but there were always latent centrifugal tendencies in a country so big as Russia, embracing so many natural regions and so many different peoples. The tsars' title, significantly, was "Tsar of all the Russias", and to this day events have reflected this diversity. Russia had always to be held together by a strong pull towards the centre if the divergences within it were not to be exploited by the enemies on the borders.

THE RUSSIAN NOBILITY

The humbling of the boyars left the ruling family isolated in its eminence. The Russian nobility was gradually brought to depend on the state on the grounds that nobility derived from service, which was indeed often rewarded in the seventeenth century with land and later with the grant of serfs. All land came to be held on the condition of service to the autocracy as defined in a Table of Ranks in 1722. This effectively amalgamated all categories of nobility into a single class. The obligations laid on noblemen by it were very large, often extending to a man's lifetime, though in the eighteenth century they came to be progressively diminished and were finally removed altogether. Nevertheless, service still continued to be the route to an automatic ennoblement, and Russian nobles never acquired quite such independence of their monarch as those of other countries. New privileges were conferred upon them but no closed caste emerged. Instead nobility grew hugely by new accessions and by natural increase. Some of its members were very poor, because there was neither primogeniture nor entail in Russia and property could be much subdivided in three or four generations. Towards the end of the eighteenth century most nobles owned fewer than a hundred serfs.

PETER THE GREAT

O F ALL IMPERIAL RUSSIA'S RULERS the one who made the most memorable use of the autocracy and most deeply shaped its character was Peter the Great. He came to the throne as a ten-year-old child and when he died something had been done to Russia which could never be quite eradicated. In one way he resembled twentieth-century strong men who have striven ruthlessly to drag traditional societies into modernity, but he was very much a monarch of his own day, his attention focused on victory in war – Russia was only at peace for one year in his entire reign – and he accepted that the road to that goal ran through westernizing and modernizing. His ambition to win a Russian Baltic coast supplied the driving force behind the reforms which would open the way to it. That he should be sympathetic to such a course may owe something to his childhood, growing up as he did in the "German" quarter of Moscow where foreign merchants and their retinues lived. A celebrated pilgrimage he made to Western Europe in 1697–8 showed that his interest in technology was real. Probably in his own mind he did not distinguish the urge to modernize Russians from the urge to free them forever from the fear of their neighbours. Whatever the exact balance of his motives, his reforms have ever since served as something of an ideological touchstone; generation after generation of Russians were to look back with awe and ponder what he had done and its meaning for

This statue, known as "The Bronze Horseman", dates from 1782 and represents Peter the Great (1672–1725). The tsar looks out over St Petersburg, the city he built as his capital and the symbol of his drive to westernize Russia.

Count Golovkin, depicted here in a portrait dating from 1720, accompanied the tsar Peter I on his trip to Western Europe. The count took charge of foreign affairs in 1706; three years later he was appointed State Chancellor of Russia.

Russia. As one of them wrote in the nineteenth century, "Peter the Great found only a blank page ... he wrote on it the words Europe and Occident."

EXPANSION UNDER PETER

Peter the Great's territorial achievement is the easiest to assess. Though he sent expeditions off to Kamchatka and the oases of Bokhara and ceased to pay to the Tatars a tribute levied on his predecessors, his driving ambition was to reach the sea to the west. For a while he had a Black Sea fleet and annexed Azov, but had to abandon it later because of distractions elsewhere, from the Poles and, above all, the Swedes. The wars with Sweden for the Baltic outlet were a struggle to the death. The Great Northern War, as contemporaries termed the last of them, began in 1700 and lasted until 1721. The world recognized that something decisive had happened when in 1709 the Swedish king's army, the best in the world, was destroyed far away from home at Poltava, in the middle of the Ukraine where its leader had sought to find allies among the Cossacks. The rest of Peter's reign drove home the point and at the peace Russia was established firmly on the Baltic coast, in Livonia, Estonia and the Karelian isthmus. Sweden's days as a great power were over; she had been the first victim of a new one.

A few years before this, the French *Almanach Royale* for the first time listed the Romanovs as one of the reigning families of Europe. Victory had opened the way to further contact with the West, and Peter had

This engraving shows the Swedish city of Stockholm during the reign of King Charles XII (1697–1718). Although Charles was a great warrior king, his persistent efforts to establish Swedish control of the Baltic were thwarted by Peter the Great of Russia.

Russian Expansion 1500–1800

Territorial expansion towards the east in the 16th century allowed Russia to control the Volga valley as far as the Caspian Sea and the trade routes towards Central Asia, at the expense of the Mongols. Then the conquest of Siberia began: by the end of the 17th century the Russians had reached the Pacific Ocean.

Russian expansion towards the south was more difficult, however, as it was opposed by the armies of the Ottoman Empire and the highly skilled Cossack warriors. Westward expansion was even more complicated – the Baltic states' naval power and military organization was still superior to that of the Russian forces. However, Russian territory was to expand towards both the south and the west from the reign of Peter the Great to the end of the 18th century. This confirmed the words that one of the 16th-century kings of Poland had once written to Elizabeth I of England:

"… in so much as you bring them [the Russians] not only merchandise, but also arms, which up until now they have not known, as well as arts and crafts; by which means they will make themselves stronger in order to vanquish all others … . For this, we who know them better, and who have them on our borders, warn other Christian princes in time, not to hand over their dignity, liberty and life, nor those of their subjects, to such a barbaric and cruel enemy."

(As quoted by H. G. Koenigsberger in *The Modern World 1500–1789*).

These maps show Russia's expansion between 1500 and 1689 (above) and between 1689 and 1812 (below).

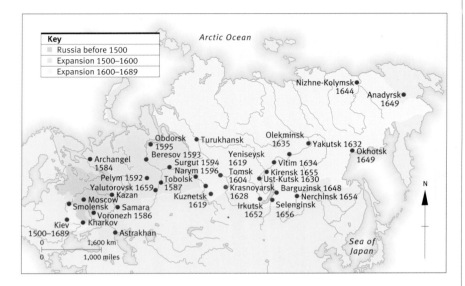

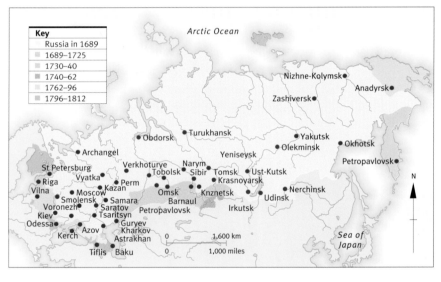

already anticipated the peace by beginning in 1703 to build, on territory captured from the Swedes, St Petersburg, the beautiful new city which was to be for two centuries the capital of Russia. The political and cultural centre of gravity thus passed from the isolation of Muscovy to the edge of Russia nearest the developed societies of the West. Now the westernizing of Russia could go ahead more easily. It was a deliberate break with the past.

WESTERNIZING RUSSIA

Even Muscovy, of course, had never been completely isolated from Europe. A pope had helped to arrange Ivan the Great's marriage, hoping he would turn to the Western Church. There was always intercourse with the neighbours, the Roman Catholic Poles, and English merchants had made their way to Moscow under Elizabeth I, where to this day they are commemorated in the Kremlin by the

In 1698 Peter the Great ordered that all boyars, noblemen and merchants cut off their traditional long beards. The consternation this caused is captured by this contemporary cartoon.

presence of a magnificent collection of the work of English silversmiths. Trade continued, and there also came to Russia the occasional foreign expert from the West. In

the seventeenth century the first permanent embassies from European monarchs were established. But there was always a tentative and suspicious response among Russians; as in later times, efforts were made to segregate foreign residents.

Peter threw this tradition aside. He wanted experts – shipwrights, gun founders, teachers, clerks, soldiers – and he gave them privileges accordingly. In administration he broke with the old assumption of inherited family office and tried to institute a bureaucracy selected on grounds of merit. He set up schools to teach technical skills and founded an Academy of Sciences, thus introducing the idea of science to Russia, where all learning had hitherto been clerical. Like many other great reformers he also put much energy into what might be thought superficialities. Courtiers were ordered to wear European clothes; the old long beards were cut back and women were told to appear in public in German fashions. Such psychological shocks

St Petersburg was founded in 1703 by Peter the Great. His new capital soon became a thriving cultural and industrial centre. This coloured engraving, entitled *View of the Neva, the Harbour and the Exchange at St Petersburg*, dates from 1815.

were indispensable in so backward a country. Peter was virtually without allies in what he was trying to do and in the end such things as he achieved had to be driven through. They rested on his autocratic power and little else. The old Duma of the boyars was abolished and a new senate of appointed men took its place. Those who resisted were ruthlessly broken, but it was less easy for Peter to dispose of a conservative cast of mind; he had at his disposal only an administrative machine and communications that would seem inconceivably inadequate to any modern government.

The most striking sign of successful modernization was Russia's new military power. More complicated tests are harder to come by. The vast majority of Russians were untouched by Peter's educational reforms, which only obviously affected technicians and a few among the upper class. The result was a fairly westernized higher nobility, focused at St Petersburg; by 1800 its members were largely French-speaking and in touch with the currents of thought which arose in Western Europe. But they were often resented by the provincial gentry and formed a cultural island

in a backward nation. The mass of the nobility for a long time did not benefit from the new schools and academies. Further down the social scale, the Russian masses remained illiterate; those who learnt to read did so for the most part at the rudimentary level offered by the teaching of the village priest, often only one generation removed from illiteracy himself. A literate Russia had to wait for the twentieth century.

SERFDOM IN RUSSIA

Russia's social structure, too, tended more and more to mark her off. She was to be the last country in Europe to abolish serfdom; among Christian countries only Ethiopia and the United States kept bonded labour for longer. While the eighteenth century saw the institution weakening almost everywhere, in Russia it spread. This was largely because labour was always scarcer than land; significantly, the value of a Russian estate was usually assessed in the number of "souls" – that is, serfs – tied to it, not its extent. The

Dating from 1815, this engraving of a military parade taking place in front of the imperial palace in St Petersburg illustrates the westernized dress of both the troops and the upper-class civilians watching the proceedings.

The Russian artist Mikhail Shibanov came from a Serb family. He specialized in depicting peasant life. *The Betrothal* shows a scene from the celebration of a marriage contract and dates from 1789.

number of serfs had begun to go up in the seventeenth century, when the tsars found it prudent to gratify nobles by giving them land, some of which already had free peasants settled on it. Debt tied them to their landlords and many of them entered into bondage to the estate to work it off. Meanwhile, the law imposed more and more restrictions on the serf and rooted the structure of the state more and more in the economy. Legal powers to recapture and restrain serfs were steadily increased and landlords had been given a special interest in using such powers when Peter had made them responsible for the collection of the poll-tax and for military conscription. Thus, economy and administration were

Reigns of the tsars and tsarinas of Russia (1462–1825)

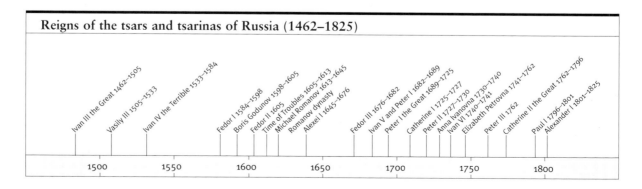

bound together in Russia more completely than in any Western country. Russia's aristocrats tended to become hereditary civil servants, carrying out tasks for the tsar.

Formally, by the end of the eighteenth century, there was little that a lord could not do to his serfs short of inflicting death on them. If they were not obliged to carry out heavy labour services, money dues were levied upon them almost arbitrarily. There was a high rate of desertion, serfs making for Siberia or even volunteering for the galleys. About a half of the Russian people were in bondage to their lords in 1800, a large number of the rest owing almost the same services to the Crown and always in danger of being granted away to nobles by it.

As new lands were annexed, their populations, too, passed into serfdom even if they had not known it before. The result was a huge inertia and a great rigidifying of society. By the end of the century, Russia's greatest problem for the next hundred years was already there: what to do with so huge a population when both economic and political demands made serfdom increasingly intolerable, but when its scale presented colossal problems of reform. It was like the man riding an elephant; it is all right so long as he keeps going but there are problems when he wants to get off.

POPULATION AND ECONOMY

Servile labour had become the backbone of the economy. Except in the famous Black Earth zone, only beginning to be opened up in the eighteenth century, Russian soil is by no means rich, and even on the best land farming methods were poor. It seems unlikely that production ever kept pace with population until the twentieth century though periodic famine and epidemics were the natural

restoratives of balance. Population nearly doubled in the eighteenth century, about seven million of the thirty-six million or so at which it stood at the end having been acquired with new territories, the rest having accumulated by natural increase. This was a faster rate of growth than in any other European country. Of this population, only about one in twenty-five at most lived in towns.

Yet the Russian economy made striking progress during the century and was unique in utilizing serfdom to industrialize. Here, it may be thought, was one of Peter's unequivocal successes; though there had been

A Russian peasant woman in festive dress is depicted in this portrait dating from 1784.

beginnings under the first two Romanovs, it was he who launched Russian industrialization as a guided movement. True, the effect was not quickly apparent. Russia's starting level was very low, and no eighteenth-century European economy was capable of rapid growth. Though grain production went up and the export of Russian cereals (later a staple of Russian foreign trade) began in the eighteenth century, it was done by the old method of bringing more land under cultivation and perhaps by the more successful appropriation of the surplus by the landlord and tax-collector. The peasant's consumption

declined. This was to be the story throughout most of the imperial era and sometimes the load was crushing: it has been estimated that taxes took 60 per cent of the peasant's crop under Peter the Great. The techniques were not there to increase productivity and the growing rigidity of the system held it down more and more firmly. Even in the second half of the nineteenth century the typical Russian peasant wasted what little time was left to him after work for his lord by trudging around the collection of scattered strips which made up his holding. Often he had no plough, and crops had to be raised from the shallow scratching of the soil which was all that was possible.

None the less, this agricultural base somehow supported both the military effort which made Russia a great power, and the first phase of her industrialization. By 1800 Russia produced more pig-iron and exported more iron ore than any other country in the world. Peter, more than any other man, was responsible for this. He grasped the importance of Russia's mineral resources and built the administrative apparatus to grapple with them. He initiated surveys and imported the miners to exploit them. By way of incentive, the death penalty was prescribed for landlords who concealed mineral deposits on their estates or tried to prevent their use. Communications were developed to allow access to these resources and slowly the centre of Russian industry shifted towards the Urals. The rivers were crucial. Only a few years after Peter's death the Baltic was linked by water to the Caspian.

INDUSTRIALIZATION

Manufacturing grew up around the core of extractive mineral and lumber industry which ensured Russia a favourable balance of trade

This portrait of a member of the Russian Demidov family was painted in 1773. The Demidovs' wealth came from the mining companies and metal works they owned in the Urals and in Siberia.

As Empress of Russia, the daughter of Peter the Great and Catherine I, Elizabeth Petrovna (1709–1762), continued her parents' policies of economic reform and waged war against Sweden and Prussia. This portrait of the empress on horseback was painted in 1743.

owners, the need of such encouragement shows that the stimuli for maintained growth which were effective elsewhere were lacking in Russia.

PETER'S SUCCESSORS

After Peter, in any case, there was a notable flagging of state innovation. The impetus could not be maintained; there were not enough educated men to allow the bureaucracy to keep up the pressure once his driving power had gone. Peter had not named a successor (he had his own son tortured to death). Those who followed him faced a renewed threat of hostility from the great noble families without his force of character and the terror he had inspired. The direct line

for the whole century. Less than a hundred factories in Peter's reign became more than three thousand by 1800. After 1754, when internal customs barriers were abolished, Russia was the largest free-trade area in the world. In this, as in the granting of serf labour or of monopolies, the state continued to shape the Russian economy; Russian industry did not emerge from free enterprise, but from regulation, and this had to be, for industrialization ran against the grain of Russian social fact. There might be no internal customs barriers, but nor was there much long-distance internal trade. Most Russians lived in 1800 as they had done in 1700, within self-sufficient local communities depending on their artisans for a small supply of manufactures and hardly emerging into a money economy. Such "factories" as there were seem sometimes to have been little more than agglomerations of artisans. Over huge areas labour service, not rent, was the basis of tenure. Foreign trade was still mainly in the hands of foreign merchants. Moreover, though state grants to exploit their resources and allocations of serfs encouraged mine-

During the reign of Elizabeth Petrovna, the Italian architect Bartolomeo Rastrelli was commissioned to build the Winter Palace in St Petersburg. The work was carried out between 1754 and 1762, and the result is shown in this engraving from 1891.

This 18th-century portrait of Catherine the Great (1729–1796) shows the empress in traditional Russian dress.

twenty years later) in favour of Elizabeth, daughter of Peter the Great, who relied on the support of the Guards regiments and Russians irritated by foreigners. She was succeeded in 1762 by a nephew who reigned barely six months before he was forced to abdicate. The mistress of the overmighty subject who subsequently murdered the deposed tsar was the new tsarina and widow of the deposed victim, a German princess who became Catherine II and known, like Peter, as "the Great".

CATHERINE THE GREAT

THE GLITTER WITH WHICH Catherine the Great surrounded herself masked a great deal and took in many of her contemporaries. Among the things it almost hid was the bloody and dubious route by which she came to the throne. It is probably true, though, that she rather than her husband might have been the victim if she had not struck first. In any case, the circumstances of her accession and of those of her predecessors showed the weakening the autocracy had undergone since Peter. The first part of her reign was a ticklish business; powerful interests existed to exploit her mistakes and for all her identification with her new country (she had renounced her Lutheran religion to become Orthodox) she was a foreigner. "I shall perish or reign," she once said, and reign she did, to great effect.

was broken in 1730 when Peter's grandson died. Yet factional quarrels could be exploited by monarchs, and his replacement by his niece, Anna, was something of a recovery for the Crown. Though put on the throne by the nobles who had dominated her predecessor, she quickly curbed them. Symbolically, the court returned to St Petersburg from Moscow, to which (to the delight of the conservatives) it had gone after Peter's death. Anna turned to foreign-born ministers for help and this worked well enough until her death in 1740. Her successor and infant grand-nephew was within a year set aside (to be kept in prison until murdered more than

Though Catherine's reign was more spectacular than that of Peter the Great, its innovatory force was less. She, too, founded schools and patronized the arts and sciences. The difference was that Peter was concerned with practical effect; Catherine rather to associate the prestige of enlightened thinkers with her court and legislation. The forms were often forward-looking while the reality was reactionary. Close observers were not taken in by legislative rhetoric; the reality was shown by the exile of the young Radischev, who had dared to criticize the régime and has been seen as Russian's first dissentient intellectual. Such reforming impulses as Catherine showed perceptibly weakened as the reign went on and foreign considerations distracted her.

The Cossack Yemelian Pugachev led an uprising in southern Russia while claiming to be Peter III, Catherine the Great's assassinated husband. Pugachev was eventually captured and was executed in 1775.

Her essential caution was well shown by her refusal to tamper with the powers and privileges of the nobility. She was the tsarina of the landlords, giving them greater power over the local administration of justice and taking away from their serfs the right to petition against their masters. Only twenty times in Catherine's thirty-four year reign did the government act to restrain landlords abusing their powers over their serfs. Most significant of all, the obligation to service was abolished in 1762 and a charter of rights was later given to the nobility which sealed a half-century of retreat from Peter's policies towards them. The gentry were exempted from personal taxation, corporal punishment and billeting, could be tried (and be deprived of their rank) only by their peers, and were given the exclusive right to set up factories and mines. The landowner was in a sense taken into partnership by the autocracy.

SOCIAL OSSIFICATION

In the long run the close relationship between the nobility and the autocracy was pernicious. Under Catherine, Russia began to truss herself more and more tightly in the corset of her social structure at a time when other countries were beginning to loosen theirs. This would increasingly unfit Russia to meet the challenges and changes of the next half-century. One sign of trouble was the scale of serf revolt. This had begun in the seventeenth century, but the most frightening and dangerous crisis came in 1773, the rebellion of Pugachev, the worst of the great regional uprisings which studded Russian agrarian history before the nineteenth century. Later, better policing would mean that revolt was usually local and containable, but it continued through almost the whole of the imperial era. Its recurrence is hardly surprising. The load of labour services piled on the peasant rose sharply in the Black Earth zone during Catherine's reign. Soon critics would appear among the literate class and the condition of the peasant would be one of their favourite themes, thus providing an early demonstration of a paradox evident in many developing countries in the next two centuries. It was becoming clear that modernization was more than a matter of technology; if you borrowed Western ideas, they could not be confined in their effect. The first critics of Orthodoxy and autocracy were beginning to appear. Eventually the need to preserve an ossifying social system would virtually bring to a halt the changes which Russia needed to retain the place that courageous and unscrupulous leadership and seemingly inexhaustible military manpower had given her.

CATHERINE'S LEGACY

By 1796, when Catherine died, Russia's position was indeed impressive. The most solid ground of her prestige was her armies and diplomacy. She had given Russia seven million new subjects. She said she had been well treated by Russia, to which she had come "a poor girl with three or four dresses", but that she had paid her debts to it with Azov, the Crimea and the Ukraine. This was in the line of her predecessors. Even when the monarchy was weak, the momentum of Peter's reign carried the foreign policy of Russia forward along two traditional lines of thrust, into Poland and towards Turkey. It helped that Russia's likely opponents laboured under growing difficulties for most of the eighteenth century. Once Sweden was out of the running, only Prussia or the Habsburg empire could provide a counter-weight, and since these two were often at loggerheads Russia could usually have her own way both over an ailing Poland and a crumbling Ottoman Empire.

PRUSSIA

IN 1701 THE ELECTOR OF BRANDENBURG, with the consent of the emperor, became a king; his kingdom, Prussia, was to last until 1918. The Hohenzollern dynasty had provided a continuous line of electors since 1415, steadily adding to their ancestral domains, and Prussia, then a duchy, had been united to Brandenburg in the sixteenth century, after a Polish king had ousted the Teutonic Knights who ruled it. Religious toleration had been Hohenzollern policy after an elector was converted to Calvinism in 1613, while his subjects remained Lutheran. One problem facing the Hohenzollerns was the spread and variety of their lands, which stretched from East Prussia to the west bank of the Rhine. The Swedes provided infilling for this scatter of territories in the second half of the seventeenth century, though there were setbacks even for the "Great Elector", Frederick William, the creator of the Prussian standing army and winner of the victories against the Swedes which were the basis of the most enduring military tradition in modern European history. Arms and diplomacy continued to carry forward his successor to the kingly crown he coveted and to participation in the Grand Alliance against Louis XIV. Prussia was by that fact alone clearly a power. This imposed a heavy cost but careful housekeeping had again built up the best army and one of the best-filled treasuries in Europe by 1740, when Frederick II came to the throne.

FREDERICK II

Frederick II was to be known as "the Great" because of the use he made of Prussia's wealth and fine army, largely at the expense of the Habsburgs and the kingdom of Poland, though also at the expense of his own people whom he subjected to heavy taxation and exposed to foreign invasion. It is difficult to decide whether he was more or less attractive than his brutal father (whom he hated), for he was malicious, vindictive and completely

Frederick William of Prussia (1620–1688), depicted in this 18th-century portrait, was victorious in the Thirty Years' War, acquiring Magdeburg and Pomerania. He went on to create a centralized adminis-tration, with close links to the army and the landowning nobility (known as "the Junkers").

This 18th-century painting shows Frederick the Great of Prussia (1712–1786), accompanied by the Marquis of Argens, visiting the construction site of the Sans-Souci Palace in Potsdam.

without scruple. But he was highly intelligent and much more cultivated, playing and composing for the flute, and enjoying the conversation of clever men. He was also utterly devoted to the interests of his dynasty, which he saw as the extension of its territories and the magnification of its prestige.

Frederick gave up some possessions too remote to be truly incorporated in the state, but added to Prussia more valuable territories. The opportunity for the conquest of Silesia came when the emperor died in 1740 leaving a daughter, whose succession he had sought to assure but whose prospects were uncertain. This was Maria Theresia. She remained Frederick's most unforgiving opponent until her death in 1780 and her intense personal dislike for him was fully reciprocated. A general European war "of the Austrian Succession" left Prussia holding Silesia. It was not to be lost in later wars and in the last year of his reign Frederick formed a

This 18th-century engraving shows the centre of Vienna, capital of Austria.

League of German Princes to thwart the attempts of Maria Theresia's son and successor, Joseph II, to negotiate the acquisition of Bavaria as a recompense for the Habsburg inheritance.

This episode matters more to European history as a whole than might be expected of a contest for a province, however rich, and for the leadership of the princes of Germany. At first sight a reminder of how alive still in the eighteenth century were the dynastic preoccupations of the past, it is also, and more importantly, the opening of a theme with a century of life to it, and consequences great for Europe. Frederick launched a struggle between Habsburg and Hohenzollern for the mastery of Germany which was only to be settled in 1866. That is further ahead than may be usefully considered at present; but this context gives perspective to the Hohenzollern appeal to German patriotic sentiment against the emperor, many of whose essential interests were non-German. There would be periods of good relations, but in the long struggle which began in 1740 Austria's great handicap would always be that she was both more and less than a purely German state.

THE CRIMEA

The disadvantages of the spread of Maria Theresia's interests were made very obvious during her reign. The Austrian Netherlands were an administrative nuisance rather than a strategic advantage, but it was in the east that the worst distractions from German problems arose, and they became increasingly pressing as the second half of the century brought more and more clearly into view the likelihood of a long and continuing confrontation with Russia over the fate of the Ottoman Empire. For thirty years or so Russo-Turkish relations had been allowed to slumber with only occasional minor eruptions over the building of a fort or the raids of the Crimean Tatars, one of the peoples originating in a fragment of the Golden Horde and under Turkish suzerainty. Then, between 1768 and 1774, Catherine fought her most successful war. A peace treaty with the Ottomans signed in an obscure Bulgarian village called Kutchuk Kainarji was one of the most important of the whole century. The Turks gave up their suzerainty over the Crimean Tatars (an important loss both materially, because of their military manpower, and morally, because this was the first Islamic people over which the Ottoman Empire ceded control), and Russia took the territory between the Bug and Dnieper, together with an indemnity, and the right of free navigation on the Black Sea and through the straits. In some ways the most pregnant with future opportunity of the terms, was a right to take up with the Turks the interests of "the church to be built in Constantinople and those who serve it". This meant that the Russian government was recognized as the guarantor and protector of new rights granted to the Greek – that is, Christian – subjects of the Sultan. It was to prove a blank cheque for Russian interference in Turkish affairs.

Almost at once it became clear that this was a beginning, not an end. In 1783 Catherine annexed the Crimea, and after another war with the Turks her armies carried her frontier up to the line of the Dniester. The next obvious boundary ahead was the Pruth, which meets the Danube a hundred miles or so from the Black Sea. The possibility of Russia's installation at the mouth of the Danube was to remain an Austrian nightmare, but the danger which appeared in the east before this was that Russia would swallow Poland. With the eclipse of Sweden, Russia had effectively had her own way at Warsaw, happy to leave her interests to be secured through a compliant Polish king. The factions of the magnates and their quarrels blocked the road to reform and without reform Polish independence would be a fiction because effective resistance to Russia was impossible. When there seemed to be for a moment a slight chance of reforms these were checkmated by skilful Russian exploitation of religious divisions to produce confederations which speedily reduced Poland to civil war.

THE PARTITIONING OF POLAND

The last phase of Poland's independent history had opened when the Turks declared war on Russia in 1768, with the excuse that they wished to defend Polish liberties. Four years later, in 1772, came the first "Partition" of Poland, in which Russia, Prussia and Austria shared between them about one-third of Poland's territory and one-half of her inhabitants. The old international system which had somewhat artificially preserved Poland had now disappeared. After two more partitions Russia had done best on the map, absorbing something like 180,000 square miles of territory (though in the next century it would be clear that the population of

dissident Poles which went with it was by no means an unambiguous gain) but Prussia also did well, emerging from the division of booty with more Slav than German subjects. Nevertheless, so huge a prize set the seal on Russian success; the transformation of Eastern Europe since 1500 was complete and the stage was set for the nineteenth century, when there would be no booty left to divert Austria and Russia from the Ottoman succession problem. Meanwhile, independent Poland disappeared for a century and a quarter.

DAWN OF A NEW AGE

Catherine rightly claimed to have done much for Russia, but she had only deployed a strength already apparent. Even in the 1730s, a Russian army had been as far west as the Neckar; in 1760 another marched into Berlin. In the 1770s there was a Russian fleet in the Mediterranean. A few years later a Russian army was campaigning in Switzerland and, after twenty years, another entered Paris. The paradox at the heart of such evidences of strength was that this military power was based on a backward social and economic structure. Perhaps this was inherent in what Peter had done. The Russian state rested on a society with which it was fundamentally incompatible, and later Russian critics would make much of this theme. Of course, this did not mean that the clock could be put back. The Ottoman Empire was for ever gone as a serious competitor for power while Prussia's emergence announced a new age as much as did Russia's. The future international weight of the United Provinces and Sweden had been unimaginable in 1500, but their importance, too, had come and gone by 1800; they were then still important nations, but of the second rank. France was still to be a front-rank power in an age of national states as she had been in the days of sixteenth-century dynastic rivalry; indeed, her power was relatively greater and the peak of her dominance in Western Europe was still to come. But she faced a new challenger, too, and one which had already defeated her. From the little English kingdom of 1500, cooped up in an island off the coast of Europe under an upstart dynasty, had emerged the world power of Great Britain.

This was a transformation almost as surprising and sudden as Russia's and it transcended the old categories of European diplomacy quite as dramatically. In three hundred years, the major zones of European conflict and dispute had migrated from the old battlegrounds of Italy, the Rhine and the Netherlands, moving from them to central and eastern Germany, the Danube valley, Poland and Carpathia, and the Baltic, but also, greatest change of all, across the oceans. A new age had indeed opened. It was signalled not only by the remaking of Eastern Europe, but in the wars of Louis XIV, the first world wars of the modern era, imperial and oceanic in their scope.

A contemporary print represents the first partition of Poland by the Eastern European monarchs, who are shown dividing the spoils.

4 *EUROPE'S ASSAULT ON THE WORLD*

THE CHANGE WHICH CAME ABOUT in world history after 1500 is quite without precedent. Never before had one culture spread over the whole globe. From the earliest observable stage of prehistory, the tendency had always been towards differentiation. Now the cultural tide was turning. The essentials of what was happening were evident even by the end of the eighteenth century. Including Russia, European nations by then already laid claim to more than half the world's land surface and, in varying degree, actually controlled about a third of it. To the western hemisphere they had by then already transplanted settler populations large enough to constitute new centres of civilization; a new nation had emerged from former British territory in North America, and to the south the Spaniards had destroyed two mature civilizations to implant their own. To the east, the story was different, but equally impressive. Once past the Cape of Good Hope (where something like 20,000 Dutch lived), an Englishman travelling on an East Indiaman in 1800 would not touch at European colonial communities like those of the Americas unless he wandered as far off course as Australia, just beginning to receive its settlers. But in East Africa, Persia, India, Indonesia he would find Europeans come to do business and then, in the long or short run, planning to return home to enjoy the profits. They could even be found in Canton, or, in very small numbers, in the closed island kingdom of Japan. Only the interior of Africa, still protected by disease and climate, seemed impenetrable.

EUROPE LOOKS OUTWARD

The remarkable transformation in world history that began with the establishment of

Geographers, such as this one portrayed by Diego Velázquez between 1624 and 1626, were highly respected figures during the 16th and 17th centuries.

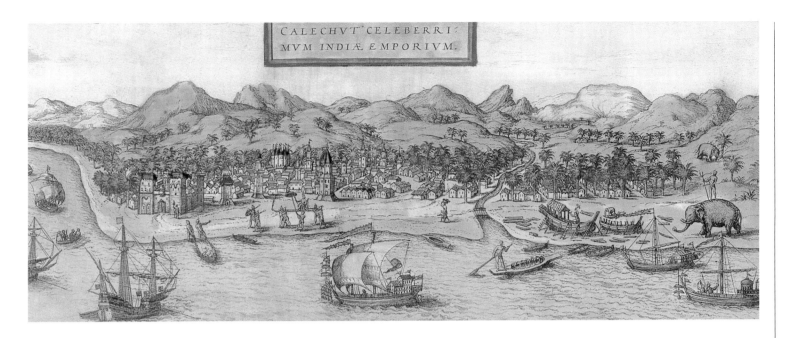

CALECHVT CELEBERRI:
MVM INDIÆ EMPORIVM.

the first European colonies (and that would go much further) was almost entirely a one-way process. Europeans went out to the world, it did not come to them. Few non-Europeans other than Turks entered Europe except as exotic imports or slaves. The Arabs and Chinese were by no means unskilful sailors. They had made oceanic voyages and knew about the compass, while the island peoples of the Pacific made long sea crossings on their mysterious errands, but the ships which came round the Horn or the tip of Africa to Atlantic ports were European and homeward bound, not Asiatic ones.

This was a great transformation of world relationships and it was the work of Europeans. Underpinning it lay layer upon layer of exploration, enterprise, technical advantage and governmental patronage. The trend seemed irreversible by the end of the eighteenth century and, in a sense, so it was to prove, even if direct European rule was to dissolve more quickly than it was built up. No civilization had been more rapidly and dramatically successful, so untroubled in its expansion by any but temporary and occasional setbacks.

MIXED MOTIVES FOR EUROPEAN EXPANSION

One advantage possessed by Europeans had been the powerful motives they had to succeed. The major thrust behind the Age of Reconnaissance had been their wish to get into easier and more direct contact with the Far East, the source of things badly wanted in Europe, at a time when the Far East wanted virtually nothing Europe could offer in exchange. When Vasco da Gama showed what he brought to give to a king, the inhabitants of Calicut laughed at him; he had nothing to offer which could compare with what Arab traders already brought to India from other parts of Asia. It was indeed just the known superiority of so much of the civilization of the Orient that spurred Europeans on to try to reach it on some more regular and assured basis than the occasional trip of a Marco Polo. Coincidentally, China, India and Japan were at something like a cultural peak in the sixteenth and seventeenth centuries. The land blockade of Europe by the Turk made them even more attractive to Europeans than they had been before. There

Calicut, in southern India, was the first Indian port to be reached by the Portuguese – Vasco da Gama landed there in 1498. This engraving shows Calicut as it was c.1572.

were huge profits to be made and great efforts could be justified.

If the expectation of reward is a good recipe for high morale, so is the expectation of success. By 1500 enough had been done for the business of exploration and new enterprise to be attacked confidently; there was a cumulative factor at work, as each successful voyage added both to knowledge and to the certainty that more could be done. As time went by, there would also be profits for the financing of future expansion. Then there was the psychological asset of Christianity. Soon after the establishment of settlement this found a vent in missionary enterprises, but it was always present as a cultural fact, assuring Europeans of their superiority to the peoples with which they began to come into touch for the first time. In the next four centuries, it was often to have disastrous effects. Confident in the possession of the true religion, Europeans were impatient and contemptuous of the values and achievements of the peoples and civilizations they disturbed. The result was always uncomfortable and often brutal. It is also true that

religious zeal could blur easily into less avowable motives. As the greatest Spanish historian of the American conquests put it when describing why he and his colleagues had gone to the Indies, they thought "to serve God and his Majesty, to give light to those who sat in darkness and to grow rich as all men desire to do".

Greed quickly led to the abuse of power, to domination and exploitation by force. In the end this led to great crimes – though they were often committed unconsciously. It sometimes brought about the destruction of whole societies, but this was only the worst aspect of a readiness to dominate present from the beginning in European enterprise. The adventurers who first reached the coasts of India were soon boarding Asian merchantmen, torturing and slaughtering their crews and passengers, looting their cargoes and burning the ravaged hulks. Europeans could usually exact what they wanted in the end because of a technical superiority which exaggerated the power of their tiny numbers and for a few centuries turned the balance against the great historic agglomerations of population.

SHIPS AND GUNS

The next Portuguese captain after da Gama to go to India provided a fitting symbol of this by bombarding Calicut. A little later, when in 1517 the Portuguese reached Canton, they fired a salute as a gesture of friendship and respect, but the noise of their guns horrified the Chinese (who at first called them *folangki* – a remote corruption of "Franks"). These weapons were much more powerful than anything China had. There had long been guns in Asia, and the Chinese had known about gunpowder centuries before Europe, but the technology of artillery had stood still there. European craftsmanship and metallurgy had in the fifteenth century made great strides, producing weapons better than any available elsewhere in the world. There were still more dramatic improvements to come, so that the comparative advantage of Europeans was to increase, right down to the twentieth century. This progress had been and was to be, again, paralleled in other fields, notably by the developments in ship-building and handling which have already been touched upon. When combined, such advances produced the remarkable weapon with which Europe opened up the world, the sailing-ship which was a gun-carrier. Again, evolution was far from complete in 1517, but already the Portuguese had been able to fight off the fleets organized by the Turks to keep them out of the Indian Ocean. (The Turks had more success in keeping control of the Red Sea, because in those narrower waters the oar-propelled galley which closed with its enemies to grapple and board retained more of its usefulness. Even there, though, the Portuguese were able to penetrate as far as the Suez isthmus.) The Chinese war-junk would do no better than the rowed galley. The abandonment of the oar for propulsion and the mounting, broadside, of large

From the *Gallery of Maps*, this illustration, which was commissioned by Pope Gregory XIII between 1580 and 1583, shows a 16th-century galleon. These sailing ships, with their fine lines, high forecastles and sternposts, were the first to mount bow-chasers – guns firing forward – as well as guns mounted traditionally, broadside.

numbers of guns, enormously multiplied the value of Europe's scanty manpower.

This European advantage was clear to contemporaries. As early as 1481 the pope forbade the sale of arms to Africans. The Dutch in the seventeenth century were very anxious to keep to themselves the secrets of gun-founding and not to allow them to pass into the hands of Asiatics. Yet pass they did. There had been Turkish gunners in India in the fifteenth century and before they reached China the Portuguese were supplying the Persians with cannon and teaching them how to cast more in order to embarrass the Turks. In the seventeenth century their knowledge of gun-founding and gunnery was one of the attractions which kept the Jesuit Fathers in favour with the Chinese authorities.

EUROPEAN CONFIDENCE

Although, as the Dutch feared, the knowledge of up-to-date gun founding penetrated oriental societies it did not offset the European advantage. Chinese artillery remained inferior in spite of the Jesuits' training. There was more to the technological disparity of Europe and the world than mere know-how. One of the assets Europe enjoyed at the beginning of her era was not only knowledge, but an attitude to knowledge different from that of other cultures. There

European trading stations and possessions in Africa and Asia c.1750

During the 17th century the Persian and Ottoman empires entered a long period of decline. The Dutch, English and French gradually replaced the Portuguese in the Indian Ocean and in Asia, where the colonial forces increased commercial exploitation. Meanwhile, the Spanish and Portuguese continued their colonization and exploitation of Central and South America, and the French, English and Dutch began to establish themselves in the West Indies and on the coasts of North America.

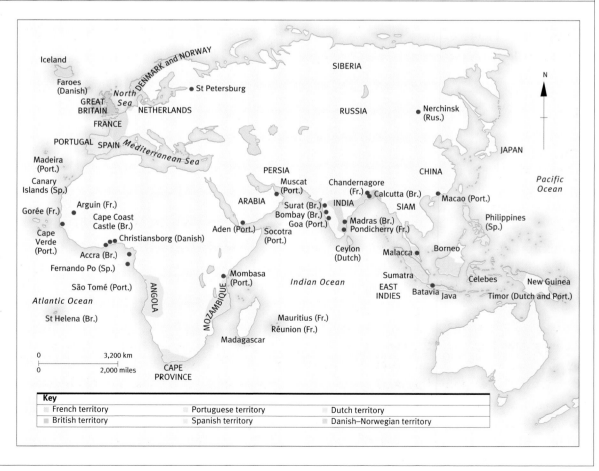

Key
| French territory | Portuguese territory | Dutch territory |
| British territory | Spanish territory | Danish–Norwegian territory |

was a readiness to bring it to bear upon practical problems, a technological instinct for the useful. In it lay the roots of another psychological characteristic of Europeans, their growing confidence in the power to change things.

Here, perhaps, was the most fundamental difference of all between them and the rest of the world. Europe was open to the future and its possibilities in a way that other cultures were not. On this confidence would long rest a psychological advantage of the greatest importance. Even in 1500 some Europeans had seen the future – and it worked.

PORTUGUESE IMPERIALISM

AFRICA AND ASIA were the first targets against which Europeans' advantages were deployed. In these continents, the Portuguese led for a century and more. They figured so largely and were so successful in the opening of routes to the East that their king took the title (confirmed by the pope) "Lord of the conquest, navigation and commerce of India, Ethiopia, Arabia and Persia", which sufficiently indicates both the scope and the eastern bias of Portuguese enterprise, but is slightly misleading in its reference to Ethiopia, with which Portuguese contacts were small. Penetration of Africa was impossible on any more than a tiny and hazardous basis. The Portuguese suggested that God had especially set a barrier about the African interior in its mysterious and noxious diseases (which were to hold Europeans at bay until the end of the nineteenth century). Even the coastal stations of West Africa were unhealthy and could only be tolerated because of their importance in the slave trade and the substructure of long-range commerce. The East African stations were less unhealthy, but they, too, were of

This 19th-century engraving is a copy of a 16th-century image of the *St Catherine of Mount Sinai*, the flagship of Vasco da Gama's squadron.

interest not as jumping-off points for the interior, but because they were part of a commercial network created by Arabs, whom the Portuguese deliberately harried so as to send up the cost of the spices purveyed by way of the Red Sea and the Middle East to the Venetian merchants of the eastern Mediterranean. The successors of the Portuguese were to leave the interior of Africa alone as they had done, and the history of that continent for another two centuries was still to move largely to its own rhythms in the obscure fastnesses of its forests and savannahs, its inhabitants only coming into corrosive and stimulating contact with Europeans at its fringes. It is also true, though, that the opening of the European age in Asia showed that none of

Africa in the early modern era

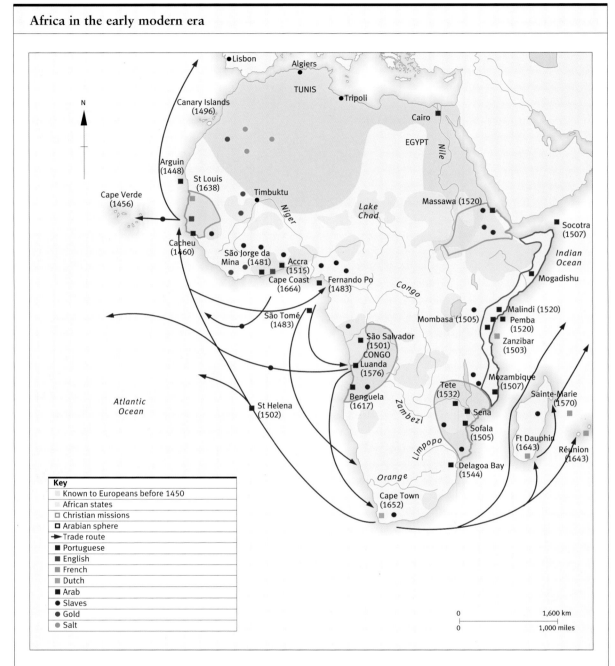

Lisbon
Algiers
TUNIS
Tripoli
Canary Islands (1496)
Cairo
EGYPT
Nile
Arguin (1448)
St Louis (1638)
Timbuktu
Massawa (1520)
Socotra (1507)
Cape Verde (1456)
Niger
Lake Chad
Indian Ocean
Cacheu (1460)
São Jorge da Mina (1481)
Accra (1515)
Cape Coast (1664)
Fernando Po (1483)
Congo
Mogadishu
São Tomé (1483)
Malindi (1520)
Pemba (1520)
Mombasa (1505)
Zanzibar (1503)
São Salvador (1501) CONGO
Luanda (1576)
Mozambique (1507)
Tete (1532)
Sainte-Marie (1570)
Atlantic Ocean
Benguela (1617)
Zambezi
Sena
Sofala (1505)
Ft Dauphin (1643)
Réunion (1643)
St Helena (1502)
Limpopo
Delagoa Bay (1544)
Orange
Cape Town (1652)

Key

	Known to Europeans before 1450
	African states
□	Christian missions
■	Arabian sphere
→	Trade route
■	Portuguese
■	English
■	French
■	Dutch
■	Arab
●	Slaves
●	Gold
●	Salt

0   1,600 km
0   1,000 miles

At the beginning of the 15th century, having Christianized various newly discovered lands and acquired profitable trade routes, the Portuguese began the exploration and colonization of the Azores and Madeira. With the encouragement of Prince Henry the Navigator, the Portuguese naval forces risked visiting the uncharted western African coast, in search of a new route towards the East, the source of the spices and wonders of which Marco Polo had written.

Spanish sailors followed the Portuguese example; the Spanish also occupied the Canary Islands. Both nations established small settlements along the African coast – secure harbours where their ships could break their journeys. By the end of the 15th century, many of these had grown into important European trading posts and power bases, and the French, English and Dutch – the great European empire-builders of the Modern Age – also had commercial interests in the region.

the powers concerned was in the first place interested in the subjugation or settlement of large areas. The period down to the middle of the eighteenth century was marked by the multiplication of trading posts, concessions in port facilities, protective forts and bases on the coast, for these by themselves would assure the only thing early imperialism sought in Asia, secure and profitable trade.

THE PORTUGUESE TRADE MONOPOLY

The Portuguese dominated trade with Asia in the sixteenth century; their fire-power swept all before them and they rapidly built up a chain of bases and trading posts. Twelve years after Vasco da Gama arrived at Calicut the Portuguese established their main Indian Ocean trading station some three hundred miles further up the western Indian coast, at Goa. It was to become a missionary as well as a commercial centre; once established, the Portuguese Empire strongly supported the propagation of the faith, and the Franciscans played a large part in this. In 1513 the first Portuguese ships reached the Moluccas, the legendary spice islands, and the incorporation of Indonesia, Southeast Asia, and islands as far south as Timor within the European horizon began. Four years later the first Portuguese ships reached China and opened direct European trade with that empire. Ten

years later they were allowed to use Macao; in 1557 they obtained a permanent settlement there. When Charles V gave up to them the rights which Spain had claimed as a result of exploration in the Moluccas, keeping only the Philippines in the Far East, and renouncing any interest in the Indian Ocean area, the Portuguese were in possession of a monopoly of eastern empire for the next half-century.

It was a trading monopoly, and not only one of trade with Europe; there was much business to be done as carriers between Asian countries; Persian carpets went to India, cloves from the Moluccas to China, copper and silver from Japan to China, Indian cloth to Siam. Both the Portuguese and their successors found this a profitable source of income to offset some of the costs of Europe's unfavourable balance of trade with Asia. For a long time Asia wanted little from Europe except silver. The only serious competitors at sea were the Arabs and they were controlled effectively by Portuguese squadrons operating from the East African bases, from Socotra, at the mouth of the Red Sea, where they had established themselves in 1507, from Ormuz, on the Muscat coast at the entrance to the Persian Gulf, and from Goa. From these places the Portuguese expanded their commerce further and eventually pushed into the Red Sea as far as Massawa and up to the head of the Persian Gulf, where they established a factory at Basra. They had also

A town in Goa is depicted in this 16th-century Dutch engraving. Goa was occupied by Affonso d'Albuquerque in 1510 and formed part of Portuguese India until 1961, when it was annexed by the Union of India.

The Portuguese traders often commissioned African artisans to produce luxury objects. This 16th-century Benin-style salt cellar is made of ivory. Figures of Portuguese warriors decorate the base, and the lid is crowned by a model of a Portuguese caravel.

secured trading privileges in Burma and Siam and in the 1540s were the first Europeans to land in Japan. This network of stations and privileges was supported by a diplomacy of agreements with local rulers and the superiority of Portuguese fire-power at sea. Even if they had wished to do so, they could not have developed this power on land because they

lacked men, so that a commercial empire was not only economic sense but was all that could be created with the means available.

PORTUGUESE WEAKNESS

Portugal's supremacy disguised fundamental weaknesses, a lack of manpower and a shaky financial base. It lasted until the end of the century and was then replaced by that of the Dutch, who carried the technique and institutions of commercial empire to their furthest development. The Dutch were the trading imperialists *par excellence*, though in the end they also carried out some settlement in Indonesia. Their opportunity arose when Portugal was united with Spain in 1580. This change provided a stimulus to Dutch seamen now excluded from the profitable re-export trade of oriental goods from Lisbon to northern Europe which had been mainly in their hands. The background of the Eighty Years' War with Spain was an additional incentive for the Dutch to enter areas where they might make profits at the expense of the Spanish. With less than two million people, their survival depended on a narrow base; commercial wealth was therefore vitally important to them. They had large advantages in the pool of naval manpower, ships, wealth and experience built up by their ascendancy in fishing and carrying in northern waters, and commercial expertise at home made it easy to mobilize resources for new enterprises. The Dutch were assisted, too, by the simultaneous recovery of the Arabs, who took back the East African stations north of Zanzibar as Portuguese power wavered in the aftermath of the Spanish union.

The first decades of the seventeenth century brought the collapse of much of the Portuguese Empire in the East and its replacement by the Dutch. The main objective of the

Dutch was the Moluccas. A brief period of individual voyages (sixty-five in seven years, some round the Straits of Magellan, some round Africa) ended when in 1602, at the initiative of the States General, the government of the United Provinces, there was set up the Dutch United East India Company, the organization which was to prove the decisive instrument of Dutch commercial supremacy in the East. Like the Portuguese before them, the company's servants worked through diplomacy with native rulers to exclude competitors, and through a system of trading stations. How unpleasant the Dutch could be to rivals was shown in 1623, when ten Englishmen were murdered at Amboyna; this ended any English attempt to intervene directly in the spice trade. Amboyna had been one of the first Portuguese bases to be seized in a rapid sweeping-up of Portuguese interests, but it was not until 1609, when a resident governor-general was sent to the East, that the reduction of the major Portuguese forts could begin. The centre of these operations was the establishment of the Dutch headquarters at Jakarta (renamed Batavia) in Java, where it was to remain until the end of Dutch colonial rule. It became the centre of an area of settlement, where Dutch planters could rely upon the company to back them up in a ruthless control of their labour force. The early history of the Dutch colonies is a grim one of insurrection, deportation, enslavement and extermination. The trade of

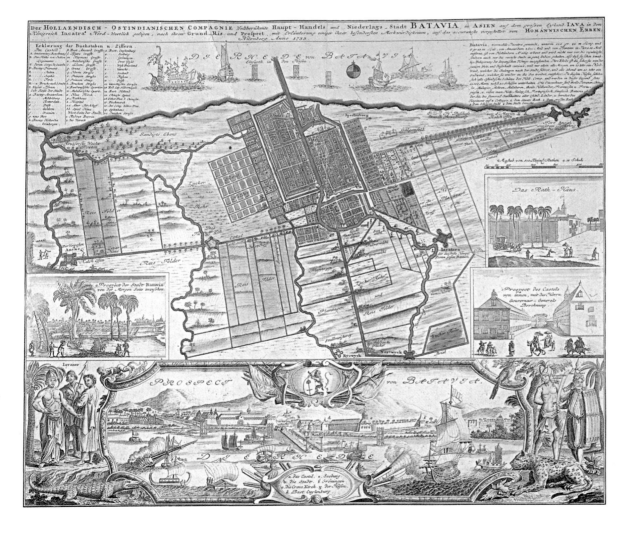

This 18th-century engraving shows Batavia (Jakarta), the capital of the Dutch colony on the Indonesian island of Java and site of the headquarters of the Dutch East India Company.

local shippers – and of the Chinese junks – was deliberately destroyed in order to concentrate all sources of profit in the hands of the Dutch.

DUTCH TRADE

The spice trade to Europe was the centre of Dutch attention and was a huge prize. It accounted during most of the century for over two-thirds of the values of the cargoes sent back to Amsterdam. But the Dutch also set about replacing the Portuguese in the valuable East Asian trade. They could not expel the Portuguese from Macao, though they sent expeditions against it, but succeeded in setting themselves up in Formosa, from which they built up an indirect trade with the mainland of China. In 1638 the Portuguese were expelled from Japan and the Dutch succeeded them there. In the next two decades, the Portuguese were replaced by the Dutch in Ceylon, too. Their successful negotiation of a monopoly of trade to Siam, on the other hand, was overtaken by another power, France. This country's connexion with the area was opened by accident in 1660 when circumstance took three French missionaries to the Siamese capital. Thanks to their establishment of a mission centre and the presence of a Greek adviser at the Siamese court there followed a French diplomatic and military mission in 1685. But these promising beginnings ended in civil war and failure and Siam moved again out of the sphere of European influence for another two centuries.

In the early eighteenth century there thus existed a Dutch supremacy in the Indian Ocean and Indonesia, and an important Dutch interest in the China seas. To a remarkable degree this reproduced the earlier Portuguese pattern, although there survived Portuguese stations such as Goa and Macao. The heart of Dutch power was the Malacca Strait, from which it radiated through Malaysia and Indonesia, to Formosa and the trading links with China and Japan, and down to the southeast to the crucial Moluccas. This area was by now enjoying an internal trade so considerable that it was beginning to be self-financing, bullion from Japan and China providing its flow of currency rather than bullion from Europe as in the early days. Further west, the Dutch were also established at Calicut, in Ceylon and at the Cape of Good Hope, and had set up factories in Persia. Although Batavia was a big

A contemporary oil painting shows the fleet of the Dutch East India Company returning to the port of Amsterdam in the early 17th century, carrying spices and other valuable commodities from the East.

A delegation from the Dutch United East India Company is shown visiting Hooghly in Bengal in this 17th-century painting.

town and the Dutch were running plantations to grow the goods they needed, this was still a littoral or insular commercial empire, not one of internal dominion over the mainland. In the last resort it rested on naval power and it was to succumb, though not to disappear, as Dutch naval power was surpassed.

THE ENGLISH IN INDIA

DUTCH NAVAL SUPERIORITY was clearly beginning to be threatened in the last decades of the seventeenth century. The unlikely challenger for Indian Ocean supremacy was England. At an early date the English had sought to enter the spice trade. There had been an East Indian Company under James I, but its factors had got bloody noses for their pains, both when they tried to cooperate with the Dutch and when they fought them. The upshot of this was that by 1700 the English had in effect drawn a line under their accounts east of the Malacca

Strait. Like the Dutch in 1580, they were faced with a need to change course and did so. The upshot was the most momentous event in British history between the Protestant Reformation and the onset of industrialization, the acquisition of supremacy in India.

In India the main rivals of the English were not the Dutch or Portuguese, but the French. What was at stake did not emerge for a long time. The rise of British power in India was very gradual. After the establishment of Fort St George at Madras and the acquisition of Bombay from the Portuguese as a part of the dowry of Charles II's queen, there was no further English penetration of India until the end of the century. From their early footholds (Bombay was the only territory they held in full sovereignty) Englishmen conducted a trade in coffee and textiles less glamorous than the Dutch spice trade, but one which grew in value and importance. It also changed their national habits, and therefore society, as the establishment of coffee-houses in London showed. Soon, ships began to be sent from

This contemporary illustration depicts Akbar, the Moghul emperor of India, crossing the River Ganges. When Akbar died in 1605, his huge empire was already under threat, not only from internal religious struggles, but also from growing interference by Europeans trading in India.

India to China for tea; by 1700 the English had found their national beverage and a poet would soon commemorate what he termed "cups that cheer but not inebriate".

THE COLLAPSE OF THE MOGHUL EMPIRE

As a defeat of the East India Company's forces in 1689 showed, military domination in India was unlikely to prove easy. Moreover, it was not necessary to prosperity and the company did not wish to fight if it could avoid it. Though at the end of the century a momentous acquisition was made when the company was allowed to occupy Fort William, which it had built at Calcutta, the directors in 1700 rejected the idea of acquiring fresh territory or planting colonies in India as quite unrealistic. Yet all preconceptions were to be changed by the collapse of the Moghul Empire after the death of Aurungzebe in 1707. The consequences emerged slowly, but their total effect was that India dissolved into a collection of autonomous states with no paramount power.

The Moghul Empire had already before 1707 been troubled by the Marathas. The centrifugal tendencies of the empire had always favoured the nawabs, or provincial governors, too, and power was divided between them and the Marathas with increasing obviousness. The Sikhs provided a third focus of power. Originally appearing as a Hindu sect in the sixteenth century, they had turned against the Moghuls but had also drawn away from orthodox Hinduism to become virtually a third religion with it and Islam. The Sikhs formed a military brotherhood, had no castes, and were well able to look after their own interests in a period of disunion. Eventually a Sikh empire appeared in northwest India which was to endure until 1849. Meanwhile, there were signs in the eighteenth century of an increasing polarity between Hindu and Muslim. The Hindus withdrew more into their own communities, hardening the ritual practices which publicly distinguished them. The Muslims reciprocated. On this growing dislocation, presided over by a Moghul military and civil administration which was conservative and unprogressive, there fell also a Persian invasion in the 1730s and consequent losses of territory.

RIVALRY BETWEEN BRITAIN AND FRANCE

There were great temptations to foreign intervention in the disintegration of the Moghul Empire. In retrospect it seems remarkable that both British and French took so long to take advantage; even in the 1740s the British East India Company was still less wealthy and powerful than the Dutch. This delay is a testimony to the importance still attached to trade as their main purpose. When they did begin to intervene, largely moved by hostility to the French and fear of what they might do, the British had several important advantages. The possession of a station at Calcutta placed them at the door to that part of India which was potentially the richest prize, Bengal and the lower Ganges valley. They had assured sea communications with Europe, thanks to British naval power, and ministers listened to the East India merchants in London as they did not listen to French merchants at Versailles. The French were the most dangerous potential competitors but their government was always likely to be distracted by its European continental commitments. Finally, the British lacked missionary zeal; this was true in the narrow sense that Protestant interest in missions in

The meeting between Robert Clive and the nawab (prince) of Bengal's General Mir Jafar after the Battle of Plassey in 1757 is depicted in this painting. The British victory, which was secretly aided by Jafar, led to their acquisition of Bengal. Jafar was rewarded when the British placed him on the defeated nawab's throne.

Asia quickened later than Catholic, and also, more generally, in that they had no wish to interfere with native custom or institution but only – somewhat like the Moghuls – to provide a neutral structure of power within which Indians could carry on their lives as they wished while the commerce from which the company profited prospered in peace.

CONFLICT IN THE CARNATIC

The way into an imperial future led through Indian politics. Support for rival Indian princes was the first, indirect, form of conflict between French and British. In 1744 this led for the first time to armed struggle between British and French forces in the Carnatic, the southeastern coastal region.

India had been irresistibly sucked into the worldwide conflict between British and French power. The Seven Years' War (1756–63) was decisive. Before its outbreak, there had in fact been no remission of fighting in India, even while France and Great Britain were officially at peace after 1748. The French cause had prospered under a brilliant French governor in the Carnatic, Dupleix, who caused great alarm to the British by his extension of French power among native princes by force and diplomacy. But he was recalled to France and the French Indian company was not to enjoy the wholehearted support of the metropolitan government which it needed to emerge as the new paramount power. When war broke out again, in 1756, the nawab of Bengal attacked and captured Calcutta. His treatment of his

English prisoners, many of whom were suffocated in the soon legendary "Black Hole", gave additional offence. The East India Company's army, commanded by its employee, Robert Clive, retook the city from him, seized the French station at Chandernagore and then on 22 June 1757 won a battle over the nawab's much larger armies at Plassey, about a hundred miles up the Hooghly from Calcutta.

It was not very bloody (the nawab's army was suborned) but it was one of the decisive battles of world history. It opened to the British the road to the control of Bengal and its revenues. On these was based the destruction of French power in the Carnatic; that opened the way to further acquisitions which led, inexorably, to a future British monopoly of India. Nobody planned this. The British government, it is true, had begun to grasp what was immediately at stake in terms of a threat to trade and sent out a battalion of regular troops to help the company; the gesture is doubly revealing, both because it recognized that a national interest was involved, but also because of the tiny scale of this military effort. A very small number of European troops with European field artillery could be decisive. The fate of India turned on the company's handful of European and European-trained soldiers, and on the diplomatic skills and acumen of its agents on the spot. Upon this narrow base and the need for government in a disintegrating India was built the British Raj.

EARLY BRITISH RULE IN INDIA

In 1764 the East India Company became the formal ruler of Bengal. This had by no means been the intention of the company's directors who sought not to govern but to trade. However, if Bengal could pay for its own government, then the burden could be undertaken. There were now only a few scattered French bases; the peace of 1763 left five trading posts on condition that they were not fortified. In 1769 the French *Compagnie des Indes* was dissolved. Soon after, the British took Ceylon from the Dutch and the stage was cleared for a unique example of imperialism.

The road would be a long one and was for a long time followed reluctantly, but the East India Company was gradually drawn on by its revenue problems and by the disorder of native administrations in contiguous territories to extend its own governmental aegis. The obscuring of the company's primary commercial role was not good for business. It also gave its employees even greater opportunities to feather their own nests. This drew the interest of British politicians, who first cut into the powers of the directors of the company and then brought it firmly under the control of the Crown, setting up in 1784 a system of "dual control" in India which was to last until 1858. In the same Act were provisions against further interference in native affairs; the British government hoped as fervently as the company to avoid being dragged any further into the role of imperial power in India. But this was what happened in the next half-century, as many more acquisitions followed. The road was open which was to lead eventually to the enlightened despotism of the nineteenth-century Raj. India was quite unlike any other dependency so far acquired by a European state in that hundreds of millions of subjects were to be added to the empire without any conversion or assimilation of them being envisaged. The character of the British imperial structure would be profoundly transformed by this, and so, eventually, would be British strategy, diplomacy, external trade patterns and, even, outlook.

The growth of British power in India

Peshawar
Khyber Pass
Rawalpindi
CHINA
Indus
Brahmaputra
AFGHANISTAN
PUNJAB
Lahore
Multan
UPPER DOAB
ROHIL KHAND
NEPAL
Delhi
RAJPUTANA
JAIPUR
Agra
LOWER DOAB
OUDH
BAST
Lucknow
Khairpur
Ajmer
Jaipur
Sindhia
BENARES
Patna
BENGAL
Ganges
SIND
Jodhpur
Gwalior
BUNDEL-KHANA
BURMA
Karachi
Holkar
CHOTA NAGPUR
BIHAR
Chandernagore
Calcutta
Ahmedabad
Indore
Gaikwar
Baroda
ORISSA
Diu (Port.)
KHANDESH
Nagpur
Bhonsla
Cuttack
Daman (Port.)
BERAR
Bombay
Ahmadnagar
Poona
NIZAM'S DOMINIONS (HYDERABAD)
Bay of Bengal
Peishwa
NORTHERN CIRCARS
Hyderabad
Arabian Sea
Goa (Port.)
Masulipatam
Nizampatam
Andaman Islands
MYSORE
KANARA
Bangalore
Pulicat
Madras
Mangalore
Mysore
CARNATIC
Pondicherry
MALABAR
SALEM
Calicut
TRAVANCORE
Negapatam
Indian Ocean
Cochin
Jaffna
Quilon
Tuticorin
Trincomali
Kandy
CEYLON
1789 British
Crown Colony
Colombo
Galle

N

Key	
▪	British acquisitions under Clive 1756–67
▪	British acquisitions under Warren Hastings 1772–85 and Cornwallis 1786–93
▪	British acquisitions under Wellesley 1798–1805
●	Important British base
Holkar – Maratha princely family	
—	Maratha Confederacy
▪	State in subsidiary alliance with Britain by 1805

0   800 km
0   500 miles

The decline of the Moghul Empire and bloody battles between Muslims and Hindus facilitated the establishment of new European trading bases. The French East India Company (founded in 1664) competed with the British East India Trading Company until 1746. Anglo-French commercial disputes tended to be settled through diplomatic channels until 1744, but fighting escalated in 1754 when war broke out between the two powers in North America, the West Indies and western Africa as well as in India. In 1757 the English victory over the nawab of Bengal at the Battle of Plassey assured British ascendancy and put an end to the French expansion on Indian territory.

SPANISH CONQUISTADORES IN THE AMERICAS

Except in india and dutch indonesia, no territorial acquisitions in the East in these centuries could be compared to the vast seizures of lands by Europeans in the Americas. Columbus' landing had been followed by a fairly rapid and complete exploration of the major "West Indian" islands. It was soon clear that the conquest of American lands was attractively easy by comparison with the struggles to win north Africa from the Moors which had immediately followed the fall of Granada and the completion of the Reconquest on the Spanish mainland. Settlement rapidly made headway, particularly in Hispaniola and Cuba. The cornerstone of the first cathedral in the Americas was laid in 1523; the Spaniards, as their city-building was intended to show, had come to stay. Their first university (in the same city, Santo Domingo) was founded in 1538.

The Spanish settlers looked for land, as agriculturalists, and gold, as speculators. They had no competitors and, indeed, with the exception of Brazil, the story of the opening up of Central and South America remains Spanish until the end of the sixteenth century. The first Spaniards in the islands were often Castilian gentry, poor, tough and ambitious. When they went to the mainland they were out for booty, though they spoke as well of the message of the Cross and the greater glory of the Crown of Castile. The first penetration of the mainland had come in Venezuela in 1499. Then, in 1513, Balboa crossed the isthmus of Panama and Europeans for the first time saw the Pacific. His expedition built houses and sowed crops; the age of the conquistadores had begun. One among them whose adventures captured and held the imagination of posterity was Hernán Cortés.

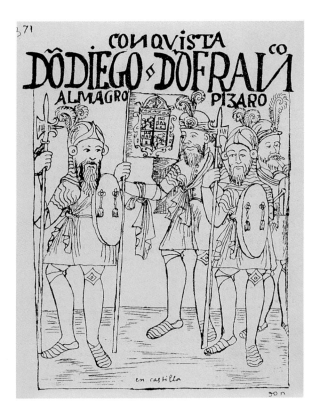

The Spanish conquistadores Diego de Almagro (1475–1538) and Francisco Pizarro (c.1475–1541) conquered the Inca Empire between 1531 and 1535 and began the Spanish colonialization of Peru. Almagro and his men went on to conquer Chile between 1535 and 1536. They then returned to Peru to dispute Pizarro's occupation of Cuzco, thus instigating a civil war between the rival Spanish forces.

CORTES AND PIZARRO

Late in 1518 Cortés left Cuba with a few hundred followers. He was deliberately flouting the authority of its governor and subsequently justified his acts by the spoils he brought to the Crown. After landing on the coast of Vera Cruz in February 1519, he burnt the ships his men had come in to ensure that they could not go back and then began the march to the high central plateau of Mexico which was to provide one of the most dramatic stories of the whole history of imperialism. When they reached the city of Mexico itself, they were astounded by the civilization they found there. Besides its wealth of gold and precious stones, it was situated in a land suitable for the kind of estate cultivation familiar to Castilians at home.

Though Cortés' followers were few and their conquest of the Aztec Empire which dominated the central plateau heroic, they had great advantages and a lot of luck. The

Royal councils, such as the one depicted in this 17th-century illustration, were gradually set up in the Spanish Americas to administer justice and to advise the Crown. With the viceroys, they formed the basic pillars of Spanish colonial administration and government.

This painting dates from 1716 and is entitled *Entry into the City of Lima of the Viceroy of Peru, Nicholas Caracciolo*. Until Charles III's reforms of 1776, the viceroy of a Spanish American colony was an extremely powerful figure. He acted as the president of the city's royal council, the captain general of the troops, the official head of the treasury and the ecclesiastical vice-patron.

people upon whom they advanced were technologically primitive, easily impressed by the gunpowder, steel and horses the conquistadores brought with them. Aztec resistance was hampered by an uneasy feeling that Cortés might be an incarnation of their god, whose return to them they one day expected. The Aztecs were very susceptible to imported diseases, too. Furthermore, they were themselves an exploiting race and a cruel one; their Indian subjects were happy to welcome the new conquerors as liberators or at least as a change of masters. Circumstances thus favoured the Spaniards. Nevertheless, in the end their own toughness, courage and ruthlessness were the decisive factors.

In 1531 Pizarro set out upon a similar conquest of Peru. This was an even more remarkable achievement than the conquest of Mexico and, if possible, displayed even more dreadfully the rapacity and ruthlessness of the conquistadores. Settlement of the new empire began in the 1540s and almost at once there was made one of the most important mineral discoveries of historical times, that of a mountain of silver at Potosí, which was to be Europe's main source of bullion for the next three centuries.

THE SPANISH EMPIRE

BY 1700, THE SPANISH EMPIRE in the Americas nominally covered a huge area from the modern New Mexico to the River Plate. By way of Panama and Acapulco it was linked by sea to the Spanish in the Philippines. Yet this huge extent on the map was misleading. The Californian, Texan and New Mexican lands north of the Rio Grande were very thinly inhabited; for the most part occupancy meant a few forts and trading posts and a large number of missions. Nor, to the south, was Chile well settled. The most important and most densely populated regions were three: New Spain (as Mexico was called), which quickly became the most developed part of Spanish America, Peru, which was important for its mines and intensively occupied, and some of the larger and long-settled Caribbean islands. Areas unsuitable for settlement by Spaniards were long neglected by the administration.

The Indies were governed by viceroys at Mexico and Lima as sister kingdoms of Castile and Aragon, dependent upon the Crown of Castile. They had a royal council of their own through which the king exercised direct authority. This imposed a high degree of centralization in theory; in practice, geography and topography made nonsense of such a pretence. It was impossible to control New Spain or Peru closely from Spain with the communications available. The viceroys and captains-general under them enjoyed an important and real independence in their day-to-day business. But the colonies could be run by Madrid for fiscal advantage and, indeed, the Spaniards and Portuguese were the only

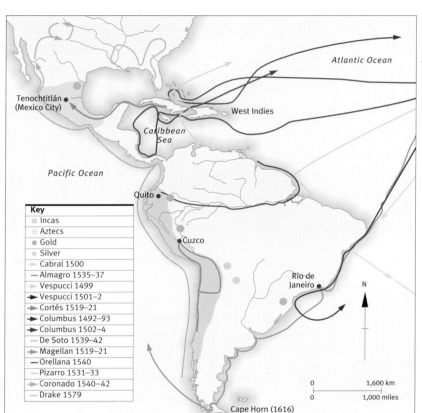

Exploration of the Americas

With the idea that the earth was spherical, the search for a sea route to the Orient began. It was this quest that led to the discovery of the American mainland by Christopher Columbus in 1498. European influence in the Americas increased significantly during the 17th century, when the acquisition of large empires in that region transformed Spain and Portugal into great powers. As a result of European colonialization in the Americas, worldwide trade increased, farming was transformed, precious metals started to flood into Europe and great population movements and mixtures began. For several centuries, America would be not only a great investment, but also a land of opportunity and hope for many Europeans.

powers colonizing in the western hemisphere for over a century which managed to make their American possessions not only pay for themselves but return a net profit for the metropolis. This was largely because of the flow of precious metals. After 1540 silver flooded across the Atlantic, to be dissipated, unfortunately for Spain, in the wars of

During the conquest of Mexico, Hernán Cortés (1485–1547) and his followers often treated the native peoples with great brutality. The Cholula people, who had refused to supply provisions to the members of a Spanish expedition, were accused of treason. Their attempts, shown in this contemporary illustration, to resist the Spanish forces were in vain: the Cholula were ruthlessly massacred.

Charles V and Philip II. By 1650, 16,000 tons of silver had come to Europe, to say nothing of 180 tons of gold objects.

THE ECONOMY OF EMPIRE

Whether Spain got economic benefits other than gold and silver bullion from her colonies is harder to say. She shared with other colonizing powers of the age the belief that there was only a limited amount of trade to go round; it followed that trade with her colonies should be reserved to her by regulation and force of arms. Furthermore, she endorsed another commonplace of early colonial economic theory, the view that colonies should not be allowed to develop industries which might reduce the opportunities available to the home country in their markets. Unfortunately, Spain was less successful than other countries in drawing advantage from this. Though they successfully prevented the development of any but extractive or handicraft industry in America, the Spanish authorities were increasingly unable to keep out foreign traders (interlopers as they came to be called) from their territories. Spanish planters soon wanted what metropolitan Spain could not supply: slaves, especially. Apart from mining, the

economy of the islands and New Spain rested on agriculture. The islands soon came to depend on black slavery; in the mainland colonies, a Spanish government unwilling to countenance the enslavement of the conquered populations evolved other devices to assure the supply of labour. The first, started in the islands and extended to Mexico, was a kind of feudal lordship: a Spaniard would be given an *encomienda*, a group of villages over which he extended protection in return for a share of their labour. The general effect was not always easily distinguishable from serfdom, or even from slavery.

THE TREATMENT OF NATIVE POPULATIONS

The presence from the start of large pre-colonial native populations to provide labour did as much as the nature of the occupying power to differentiate the colonialism of Central and South America from that of the north. Centuries of Moorish occupation had accustomed the Spanish and Portuguese to the idea of living in a multiracial society. There soon emerged in Latin America a population of mixed blood. In Brazil, which the Portuguese finally secured from the Dutch after thirty years' fighting, there was much interbreeding with the growing Negro population whose origins lay in imported slaves. (In Africa, too, the Portuguese showed no concern at racial interbreeding, and its lack of a colour bar was always a palliative feature of Portuguese imperialism.)

None the less, though the establishment of racially mixed societies over huge areas was one of the enduring legacies of the Spanish and Portuguese empires, these societies were stratified along racial lines. The governing classes were always the Iberian-born and the Creoles, persons of European blood born in the colonies. As time passed, the latter came to feel that the former, called *peninsulares*, excluded them from key posts and were antagonistic towards them. From the Creoles there led downwards a blurred incline of increasing gradations of blood to the poorest and most oppressed, and these were always the pure Indians. Though their languages survived often, and thanks to the efforts of the Spanish missionaries, the dominant languages of the continent became, of course, those of the conquerors. This was the greatest single formative influence making for the cultural unification of the continent.

Bartolomé de las Casas, the Spanish priest who fought to protect the rights of the native population in the Spanish Americas, is thought to be the figure portrayed in this 19th-century painting.

NEW WORLD CATHOLICISM

ANOTHER INFLUENCE of comparable importance to the linguistic one was the effective domination of a whole continent by Roman Catholicism. The Church played an enormous part in the opening of Spanish (and Portuguese) America. The lead was taken from the earliest years by the missionaries of the mendicant orders – Franciscans, in particular – but for three centuries their successors worked away at the civilization of native Americans. They took Indians from their tribes and villages, taught them Christianity and Latin (the early friars often kept them from learning Spanish, to protect them from corruption by the settlers), put them in trousers and sent them back to spread the light among their compatriots. The mission stations of the frontier determined the shapes of countries which would only come into existence centuries later.

For good and ill the Church saw itself from the start as the protector of the Indian subjects of the Crown. The eventual effect of this would only be felt after centuries had brought important changes in the demographic centre of gravity within the Roman communion, but it had many implications visible much earlier than this. It was in 1511 that the first sermon against the way the Spanish treated their new subjects was preached (by a Dominican) at Santo Domingo. From the start, the Spanish monarchy believed it had a moral and Christian mission in the New World. Laws were passed to protect the Indians and the advice of churchmen was sought about their rights and what could be done to secure them. But America was far away, and enforcement of laws difficult. It was all the harder to protect the native population when a catastrophic drop in its numbers created a labour shortage. The early settlers had brought smallpox to the Caribbean (its original source seems to have been Africa) and one of Cortés' men took it to the mainland; this was probably the main cause of the demographic disaster of the first century of Spanish empire in America.

The Church, meanwhile, was almost continuously seeking to convert the natives (two Franciscans baptised 15,000 Indians in a single day at Xocomilcho) and then to throw around them the protection of the mission

The English navigator Sir Francis Drake (c.1540–1596) led English pirates in attacks on Spanish and Portuguese trade monopolies in the West Indies.

without success. He brought to bear the discipline of refusing absolution even in the last rites to those whose confessions left him unsatisfied over their treatment of Indians, and argued against opponents on a thoroughly medieval basis. He assumed, with Aristotle, that some human beings were "by nature" slaves (he had black slaves of his own) but denied that the Indians were among them. He was to pass into historical memory, anachronistically, as one of the first critics of colonialism, largely because of the use made of his writings two hundred years later by a publicist of the Enlightenment.

THE CATHOLIC MONOPOLY

For centuries, the preaching and rituals of the Church were virtually the only access to European culture for the peasant, who found some of Catholicism's features sympathetic and comprehensible (the cult of the Virgin Mary, in particular, was very successful, perhaps because it was not difficult to assimilate, at least in Mexico, with indigenous tradition). To European education, only a few had access; Mexico had no native bishop until the seventeenth century, and education, except for the priesthood, did not take a peasant much further than the catechism. The Church tended, in fact, for all the devoted work of many of its clergy, to remain an imported, colonial church. Ironically, even the attempts of churchmen to protect the native Christians had the effect of isolating them (by, for instance, not teaching them Spanish) from the routes to integration with the possessors of power in their societies.

and the parish. Others did not cease to make representations to the Crown. The name of one, Bartolomé de las Casas, a Dominican, cannot be ignored. He had come out as a settler, only to become the first priest ordained in the Americas and thereafter, as theologian and bishop, he spent his life trying to influence Charles' government, and not

Perhaps this was inevitable. The Catholic monopoly in Spanish and Portuguese America was bound to mean a large measure of identification of the Church with the political structure: it was an important reinforcement for a thinly spread administrative apparatus and it was not only crusading zeal which made the Spanish enthusiastic proselytizers. The Inquisition was soon set up in New Spain and it was the Church of the Counter-Reformation which shaped American Catholicism south of the Rio Grande. This had important consequences much later; although some priests were to play important parts in the revolutionary and independence movements of South America, the Church as an organization never found it easy to adopt a progressive stance. In the long run, this meant that clericalism would become an issue in the politics of independent Latin America, where liberalism took on the associations of anti-clericalism it was to have in Catholic Europe. This was all in marked contrast to the religiously pluralistic society which appeared contemporaneously in British North America.

AGRICULTURE IN THE CARIBBEAN

For all the spectacular inflow of bullion from the mainland colonies, the New World was probably of the greatest economic importance to Europe throughout most of the early modern period because of the Caribbean islands. This importance rested on their agricultural produce, above all on sugar, introduced first by the Arabs to Europe, in Sicily and Spain, and then carried by Europeans first to Madeira and the Canaries, and then to the New World. Both the Caribbean and Brazil were transformed economically by this crop. Medieval man had sweetened his food with honey; by 1700 sugar, though still expensive, was a European necessity and was, with tobacco, hardwood and coffee, the main product of the islands. Together, these exports gave the

planters great importance in the affairs of their metropolitan countries.

The story of large-scale Caribbean agriculture began with the Spanish settlers, who quickly started growing fruit (which they had brought from Europe) and raising cattle. When they introduced rice and sugar, production was for a long time held back by a shortage of labour, as the native populations of the islands succumbed to European ill-treatment and disease. The next economic phase was the establishment by later arrivals of parasitic industries: piracy and smuggling. The Spanish occupation of the larger Caribbean islands – the Greater Antilles – still left hundreds of smaller islands unoccupied, most of them on the Atlantic fringe. These attracted the attention of English, French and Dutch captains who found them useful as bases from which to prey on Spanish ships going home from New Spain, and for contraband trade with the Spanish colonists who wanted their goods. European settlements appeared, too,

In this 18th-century engraving black slave workers are shown processing tobacco in Santo Domingo, the capital of the present-day Dominican Republic, then the Spanish colony of Hispaniola.

1. Negre qui ejambe le tabac.
2. Negre qui torque le tabac.
3. Negre qui le met en rolle.
4. Tabac a la pente.

on the Venezuelan coast where there was salt for preserving meat. Where individuals led, governmental enterprises – English royal concessions and the Dutch West India Company – followed in the seventeenth century.

ENGLISH SETTLEMENTS

By the early seventeenth century, the English had for decades been looking for suitable places for what contemporaries called "plantations" – that is, settler colonies – in the New World. They tried the North American mainland first. Then, in the 1620s they established their first two successful West Indian colonies, on St Christopher in the Leeward Isles, and Barbados. Both prospered; by 1630 St Christopher had about three thousand inhabitants and Barbados about two thousand. This success was based on tobacco, the drug which, with syphilis (first

reported in Europe at Cadiz in 1493) and the cheap automobile, was to be the New World's revenge for its disruption by the old. These tobacco colonies rapidly became of great importance to England not only because of the customs revenue they supplied, but also because the new growth of population in the Caribbean stimulated demand for exports and provided fresh opportunities for interloping in the trade of the Spanish Empire. Soon the English were joined by the French in this lucrative business, the French occupying the Windward Isles, the English the rest of the Leewards. In the 1640s there were about seven thousand French in the West Indies, and over fifty thousand English.

SUGAR AND SLAVES

After the mid-seventeenth century the tide of English emigration to the New World was

Cane sugar was one of the most profitable products traded between the New World and the Old. In the 17th century it became an affordable commodity and there was great competition among sugar producers and importers. This 17th-century engraving shows a sugar mill in the West Indies.

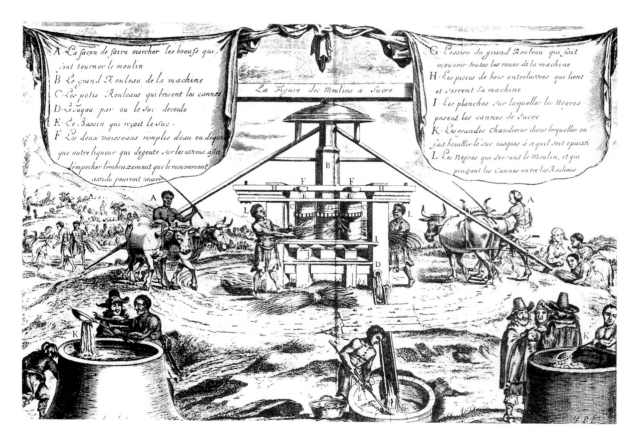

British Atlantic trade in the 1770s: the slave-trade triangle

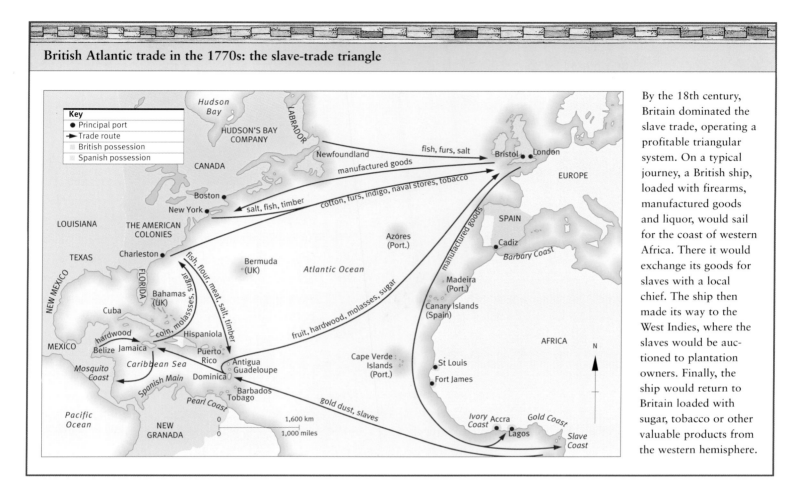

By the 18th century, Britain dominated the slave trade, operating a profitable triangular system. On a typical journey, a British ship, loaded with firearms, manufactured goods and liquor, would sail for the coast of western Africa. There it would exchange its goods for slaves with a local chief. The ship then made its way to the West Indies, where the slaves would be auctioned to plantation owners. Finally, the ship would return to Britain loaded with sugar, tobacco or other valuable products from the western hemisphere.

diverted to North America and the West Indies were not again to reach such high figures of white settlement. This was partly because sugar joined tobacco as a staple crop. Tobacco can be produced economically in small quantities; it had therefore suited the multiplication of small holdings and the building up of a large immigrant population of whites. Sugar was economic only if cultivated in large units; it suited the big plantation, worked by large numbers, and these were likely to be black slaves, given the decline of local population in the sixteenth century. The Dutch supplied the slaves and aspired to the sort of general commercial monopoly in the western hemisphere which they were winning in the Far East, working out of a base at the mouth of the Hudson river, New Amsterdam. This was the beginning of a great demographic change in the Caribbean. In 1643 Barbados had thirty-seven thousand white inhabitants and only six thousand black slaves; by 1660 there were over fifty thousand of the latter.

With the appearance of sugar, the French colonies of Guadeloupe and Martinique took on a new importance and they, too, wanted slaves. A complex process of growth was under way. The huge and growing Caribbean market for slaves and imported European goods was added to that already offered by a Spanish Empire increasingly unable to defend its economic monopoly. This set the role of the West Indies in the relationships of the powers for the next century. They were long a prey to disorder, the Caribbean an area where colonial frontiers met and policing was poor and there were great prizes to be won (in one

This 16th-century engraving shows trade ships preparing to depart from Lisbon, Portugal, bound for the West Indies, North America and Brazil.

year a Dutch captain took the great *flota* bearing home the year's treasure from the Indies to Spain). Not surprisingly, they became the classical and, indeed, legendary hunting-ground of pirates, whose heyday was the last quarter of the seventeenth century. Gradually, the great powers fought out their disputes until they arrived at acceptable agreements, but this was to take a long time. Meanwhile, through the eighteenth century the West Indies provided the great market for slaves and sustained most of that trade. As time passed, too, it became involved in another economy besides those of Europe, Africa and New Spain: that of a new North America.

NORTH AMERICA IS SETTLED

FOR A LONG TIME, by all the standards of classical colonial theory, settlement in North America was a poor second in attractiveness to Latin America or the Caribbean. Precious metals were not discovered there and

though there were furs in the north, there seemed to be little else that Europe wanted from that region. Yet there was nowhere else to go, given the Spanish monopoly to the south, and a great many nations tried it. The Spanish expansion north of the Rio Grande need not concern us, for it was hardly an occupation, but rather a missionary exercise, while Spanish Florida's importance was strategical, for it gave some protection to Spanish communications with Europe by the northern outlet from the Caribbean. It was the settlement of the Atlantic coast which drew other Europeans. There was even briefly a New Sweden, taking its place beside New Netherlands, New England and New France.

The motives for settling North America were often those which operated elsewhere, though the crusading, missionary zeal of the Reconquest mentality was almost entirely missing further north. For most of the sixteenth century the Englishmen who were the most frequent explorers of North American possibilities thought there might be mines there to rival those of the Spanish Indies. Others believed that population pressure made emigration desirable and increasing knowledge revealed ample land in temperate climates with, unlike Mexico, very few native inhabitants. There was also a constant pull in the lure of finding a northwest passage to Asia.

EUROPEAN SETTLERS

By 1600, there had been much exploration, but only one (unsuccessful) settlement north of Florida, at Roanoke, Virginia. The English were too weak, the French too distracted, to achieve more. With the seventeenth century there came more strenuous, better-organized and better-financed efforts, the discovery of the possibility of growing some important staples on the mainland, a set of political changes in England which favoured emigration, and the emergence of England as a great naval power. Between them, these facts brought about a revolutionary transformation of the Atlantic littoral. The wilderness of 1600, inhabited by a few Indians, was a hundred years later an important centre of civilization. In many places settlers had pushed as far inland as the mountain barrier of the Alleghenies. Meanwhile the French had established a line of posts along the valley of the St Lawrence and the Great Lakes. In this huge right-angle of settlement lived about a half-million white people, mainly of British and French stock.

Spain claimed all North America, but this had long been contested by the English on the ground that "prescription without possession availeth nothing". The Elizabethan adventurers had explored much of the coast and gave the name "Virginia", in honour of their queen, to all the territory north of thirty degrees of latitude. In 1606 James I granted a charter to a Virginia company to establish colonies. This was only formally the beginning; the company's affairs soon required revision of its structure and there were unprofitable initiatives in plenty, but in

1607 there was already established the first English settlement in America which was to survive, at Jamestown, in modern Virginia. It only just came through its early trials but by 1620 its "starving time" was far behind it and it prospered. In 1608, the year after Jamestown's foundation, the French explorer Samuel de Champlain built a small fort at Quebec. For the immediate future the French colony was so insecure that its food had to be brought from France, but it was the beginning of settlement in Canada. Finally, in 1609, the Dutch sent an English explorer, Henry Hudson, to find a northeast passage to Asia. When he was unsuccessful he turned completely round and sailed across the Atlantic to look for a northwestern one. Instead, he discovered the river that bears his name and established a preliminary Dutch claim by doing so. Within a few years there were Dutch settlements along the river, on Manhattan and on Long Island.

ENGLISH SUCCESSES

The English were in the lead in North America and remained so. They prospered because of two new facts. One was the

At the beginning of the 18th century, the British establishments in North America were located on a narrow coastal strip where there were still areas that had not been colonized. This 18th-century engraving shows a view of the British colony of New York.

technique, of which they were the first and most successful exponents, of transporting whole communities, men, women and children. These set up agricultural colonies which worked the land with their own labour and soon became independent of the mother country for their livelihood. The second was the discovery of tobacco, which became a staple first for Virginia and then for Maryland, a colony whose settlement began in 1634. Further north, the availability of land which could be cultivated on European lines assured the survival of the colonies; although interest in the area had originally been awoken by the prospects of fur-trading and fishery there was soon a small surplus of grain for export. This was an attractive prospect for the land-hungry English in a country widely believed in the early seventeenth century to be over-populated. Something like twenty thousand went to New England in the 1630s.

Another distinctive feature of the New England colonies was their association with religious dissent and Calvinistic Protestantism. They would not have been what they were without the Reformation. Although the usual economic motives were at work in the settlements, the leadership among immigrants to Massachusetts in the 1630s of men associated with the Puritan wing of English Protestantism bore fruit in a group of colonies whose constitutions varied from theocratic oligarchy to democracy. Though often the result of initiatives from within the English gentry and led by its members, they shed more rapidly than the southern colonies their inhibitions about radical departures from English social and political practice, and their religious nonconformity did as much as the conditions in which they had to survive to bring this about. At some moments during

The Seven Years' War for control of the French settlement of Quebec in Canada ended with the British victory at the Battle of Quebec in 1759. Under General James Wolfe, British troops sailed up the St Lawrence River and scaled steep cliffs to launch an attack on the French battalions, as shown in this contemporary engraving.

the English constitutional troubles of the mid-century it even seemed that the colonies of New England might escape from the control of the Crown altogether, but as yet this did not happen.

CANADIAN ORIGINS

After the Dutch settlements of what was subsequently New York State had been swallowed up by the English, the North American littoral in 1700 from Florida north to the Kennebec river was organized as twelve colonies (a thirteenth, Georgia, appeared in 1732). In them lived some four hundred thousand whites and perhaps a tenth of this number of black slaves. Further north lay still disputed territory and then lands that were indisputably French. In these, colonists were much thinner on the ground than in the English settlements. French North Americans numbered perhaps fifteen thousand in all and had benefited from no such large migrations of communities as had the English colonies. Many of them were hunters and trappers, missionaries and explorers, strung out over the length of the St Lawrence and dotted about in the Great Lakes region and even beyond. New France was a huge area on the map, but outside the St Lawrence valley and Quebec it was only a scatter of strategically and commercially important forts and trading posts. Nor was density of settlement the only difference between the French and English colonial zones. New France was closely supervised from home; after 1663 a company structure had been abandoned in favour of direct royal rule and Canada was governed by a French governor with the advice of the intendant much as a French province was governed at home. There was no religious liberty; the Church in Canada was monopolistic and missionary. Its history is full of

An episode from one of the first English expeditions to the Arctic is depicted in this illustration dating from 1587. The native Inuit are shown attempting to defend themselves from the European guns by firing arrows at their attackers.

glorious examples of bravery and martyrdom, and also of bitter intransigence. The farms of the settled area were grouped in *seigneuries*, a device which had some value in decentralizing administrative responsibility. Social forms therefore reproduced those of the Old World much more than those in the English settlements, even to the extent of throwing up a nobility with Canadian titles.

LIFE IN THE EARLY COLONIES

The English colonies from which were to appear the future United States of America were very diverse. Strung out as they were over almost the whole Atlantic seaboard, they contained a great variety of climate, economy and terrain. Their origins reflected a wide range of motives and methods of foundation. They were soon somewhat changed ethnically, for after 1688 Scotch, Irish, German, Huguenot and Swiss emigrants had begun to arrive in appreciable numbers, though for a very long time the predominance of the English language and the relatively small numbers of non-English-speaking immigrants would maintain a culture overwhelmingly Anglo-Saxon. There was even by 1700 a large measure of effective religious toleration, though some of the colonies had close association with specific religious denominations. Religious pluralism increased the colonies' difficulty in seeing themselves as one society. They had no American centre; the Crown and the home country were the foci of the colonies' collective life, as English culture was still their background. None the less, it was already obvious that the American colonies were different: they offered to individuals opportunities for advancement unavailable either in the more strictly and closely regulated society of Canada or at home in Europe.

By 1700, some colonies had already shown a tendency to grasp whatever independence of royal control was available to them. It is tempting to look back a long way for evidence of the spirit of independence which was later to play so big a part in popular tradition. In fact, it would be a misconception to read the prehistory of the United States in these terms. The "Pilgrim Fathers" who Landed at Cope Cod in 1620 were not rediscovered or inserted in their prominent place in the national mythology until the end of the eighteenth century. What can be seen much earlier than the idea of independence is the emergence of facts which would in the future make it easier to think in terms of independence and unity. One was the slow strengthening of a representative tradition in the first century of settlement. For all their initial diversity, in the early eighteenth century each colony settled down to work through some sort of representative assembly which spoke for its inhabitants to a royal governor appointed in London. Some of the settlements had needed to cooperate with one another against the Indians at an early date, and in the French wars this had become even more important. When the French loosed their Huron allies against the British colonists, it helped to create a sense of common interest among the individual colonies (as well as spurring on the British to enlist on their side the Iroquois who were hereditary foes of the Huron).

ECONOMICS AND GOVERNMENT

From economic diversity a measure of economic inter-relatedness was emerging. The middle and southern colonies produced the plantation crops of rice, tobacco, indigo and timber; New England built ships, refined and distilled molasses and grain spirits, grew corn and fished. There was a growing and apparent logic in thinking that the Americans might perhaps be able to run their affairs in their own interest – including that of the West Indian colonies – better than in that of the mother country. Economic growth changed the attitudes of some English immigrants, too. The northern mainland colonies of New England were on the whole underprized and even disliked in the mother country. They competed with its inhabitants in shipbuilding and, though illegally, in the Caribbean trade; unlike plantation colonies, they produced nothing that the mother country wanted. Besides, they were religious dissenters.

In the eighteenth century British America made great progress in wealth and civilization. The total colonial population had continued to grow and was well over a million by halfway through the century. As was being pointed out in the 1760s, the mainland colonies were going to be worth much more to Great Britain than the West Indies had been. By 1763, Philadelphia could rival many European cities in stylishness and cultivation. A great uncertainty had been removed in 1763, too, for Canada had been conquered and was by the peace treaty of that year to remain British. This changed the outlook of many Americans both towards the value of the protection afforded by the imperial government and towards the question of further expansion to the west. As farming settlers tended to fill up the coastal plain they came to press through the mountain barrier and down the river valleys beyond, eventually to the upper Ohio and the northwest. The danger of conflict with the French as a result was now removed, but this was not the only consideration which faced the British government in handling this movement after 1763. There were the rights and the likely reactions of the Indians to take into account. To antagonize them would be to court danger, but if Indian wars were to be avoided by holding the colonists back, then the frontier would have to be policed by British troops for that purpose, too. The result was a decision of government in London to impose a western land policy which would limit expansion, to raise taxes in the colonies to pay for the costs of defending forces, and to tighten up the commercial system and cease to wink at infringements in its working. It was unfortunate that all this was coming to a head in the last years in which the old assumptions about the economics of colonial dependencies and their relationship to the mother country were accepted without demur by the makers of colonial policy in London.

THE CONSEQUENCES OF COLONIALISM IN THE AMERICAS

By the end of the eighteenth century about two and a half centuries had gone by since European settlement in the New World began. The overall effect of expansion in the Americas upon European history had been immense, but is far from easy to define.

Eventually, it is clear, all the colonial powers had, by this time, been able to extract some economic profit from their colonies, though they did so in different ways. The flow of silver to Spain was the most obvious, but this had, of course, implications for the European economy as a whole and even for Asia. Growing colonial populations also helped to stimulate European exports and manufactures. In this respect the English colonies were of the greatest importance, pointing the way to a growing flow of emigrants from Europe which was to culminate in the last of that continent's major folk-migrations in the nineteenth and early twentieth centuries. To colonial expansion, too, must be linked the enormous growth of European shipping and shipbuilding. Whether engaged in slaving, contraband trading, legal import and export between metropolis and colony or fishing to supply new consumer markets, shipbuilders, shipowners and captains benefited. There was an incremental and incalculable effect at work. It is thus very hard to sum up the total effect of the possession of American colonies on the imperialist powers in the first age of imperialism.

Tea, coffee and chocolate from the colonies became fashionable drinks in many parts of Europe, as reflected in this 18th-century painting. The first chocolate shop in London was opened by a Frenchman in 1657.

Of the political and cultural importance of colonization it is easier to speak with confidence. Overall, the fate of the western hemisphere was to be culturally European and that meant, politically, that from Tierra del Fuego to the Hudson Bay it would eventually be organized in a series of sovereign states based on European legal and administrative principles where it did not remain directly dependent on a colonial power. It would also be Christian; when Hinduism or Islam came to the western hemisphere it would be as the possession of small minorities, not as rivals to a basically Christian culture.

THE ENGLISH INHERITANCE

More specifically, the greatest political importance of the era lay in the differentiation of America, north and south. It is not fanciful to see at the outset an ancient parallel. The ancient Greek city colonies were offshoots of parent communities not unlike the British colonies of the North American littoral. Once established, they tended to evolve towards a self-conscious identity of their own. The Spanish Empire displayed the deployment of a regular pattern of institutions essentially metropolitan and imperial, rather as had done the provinces of imperial Rome. It took time for it to be clear that the basic forms already given to the evolution of British North America were to shape the kernel of a future world power. That evolution was therefore to prove a shaper of world as well as American history. Two great transforming factors had still to operate before the North American future was fixed in its main lines; the differing environments revealed as the continent filled up by movement to the west, and a much greater flow of non-Anglo-Saxon immigration. But these forces would flow into and around moulds set by the English inheritance, which would leave its mark on the future United States as Byzantium left its own on Russia. Nations do not shake off their origins, they only learn to see them in different ways. Sometimes outsiders can see this best. It was a great German statesman who remarked towards the end of the nineteenth century that its most important international fact had been that Great Britain and the United States spoke the same language.

The British American colonies' economic resources in the 18th century

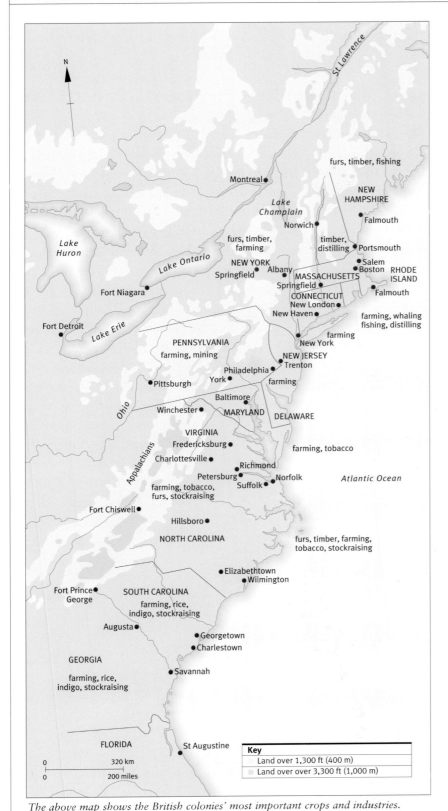

The above map shows the British colonies' most important crops and industries.

Population growth and high birth rates in North America throughout the 18th century (in 1763 there were around two million inhabitants) allowed large areas of land to be colonized, stimulating economic growth. At the beginning of the century, the North American economy was based on subsistence farming. However, by 1750, much settled land was given over to the cultivation of cash crops for export to a world market.

Although wheat was a staple in all of them, the 13 colonies in British America developed very diverse economies. The New England colonies' forests and streams supported fur and timber industries; the latter, combined with the region's natural harbours, produced a major shipbuilding industry. Fishing and whaling were similarly important. Pennsylvania was one of the richest colonies by the end of the 18th century, mainly due to the high levels of immigration to the fertile Delaware valley. The middle colonies produced grain and flour for export, while in the southern colonies large plantations, usually run on slave labour, became commonplace. The exception to this was North Carolina, cut off from international trade by its harsh coastline, where small farms were prevalent. This colony also became an important supplier of naval stores. South Carolina's more navigable coastline meant that it enjoyed trade with England and the West Indies, producing rice and, from 1742, indigo for export around the world. (Entrepreneurs in both Georgia and the Carolinas tried and failed to produce silk.) The economies of Virginia and Maryland were almost entirely reliant on tobacco which had been introduced there in the early 17th century. Both colonies were hit hard by the British Navigation Act of 1760, which stated that tobacco could be exported only to Britain.

By 1770, the total value to Great Britain of export from the North American colonies exceeded £1,000,000 sterling per annum – almost four times the total value of export in 1710.

5 WORLD HISTORY'S NEW SHAPE

IN 1776 THERE BEGAN IN AMERICA the first of a series of colonial revolts which were to take several decades to work themselves out. Besides marking an epoch in the history of the American continents these upheavals also provide a convenient vantage-ground from which to consider the first phase of European hegemony as a whole. In other parts of the world, too, something of a change of rhythm was marked by such facts as the elimination of serious French competition to the British in India, and the opening of Australasia, the last discovered and habitable continent, to settlement. At the end of the eighteenth century there is a sense of completing one era and opening another; it is a good point for assessment of the difference made by the previous three centuries to the history of the globe.

ATLANTIC EUROPE'S IMPERIALISM

Between the sixteenth and eighteenth centuries, outright conquest and occupation were the main form of European hegemony. They provided wealth Europe could use to increase still further its relative superiority over other civilizations and they set up political structures which diffused other forms of European influence. They were the work of a handful of European states which were the first world powers in the geographical range of their interests, even if not in their strength: the Atlantic nations to which the age of discoveries had given opportunities and historical destinies distinct from those of other European states.

The first to seize these opportunities had been Spain and Portugal, the only great

In 1503 the House of Contracts in Seville, Spain, was founded to deal with trade and navigation with Africa and the East. Officials here controlled virtually every aspect of this trade, including commercial traffic, the organization of the fleets, the payment and supervision of port entry taxes and nautical training. They also acted as mediators in trade disputes.

OVERSEAS ISSUES IN DIPLOMACY

colonial powers of the sixteenth century. They had long passed their zenith by 1763, when the Peace of Paris which ended the Seven Years' War was signed. This treaty is a convenient marker of a new world order which had already replaced that dominated by Spain and Portugal. It registered the ascendancy of Great Britain in the rivalry with France overseas which had preoccupied her for nearly three-quarters of a century. The duel was not over, and the French could still be hopeful that they would recover lost ground. Great Britain, none the less, was the great imperial power of the future. These two nations had eclipsed the Dutch, whose empire had been built, like theirs, in the seventeenth century, in the era of declining Portuguese and Spanish power. But Spain, Portugal and the United Provinces all still held important colonial territories and had left enduring marks on the world map.

The five major European colonial nations had by the eighteenth century been differentiated by their oceanic history from the landlocked states of central Europe or those of the Mediterranean so important in earlier centuries. Their special colonial and overseas trade interests had given their diplomats new causes and places over which to compete. Most other states had been slower to recognize how important issues outside Europe might be, and so, indeed, had even some of these five at times. Spain had fought grimly enough first for the Habsburgs in Italy, then against the Ottomans, and finally for European supremacy in the Thirty Years' War, to waste the treasure of the Indies in the process. In their long duel with the British, the French were always more liable than their rivals to distraction and the diversion of their

This engraving, entitled *The Discoveries of Captain Cook and de la Pérouse*, dates from c.1798. After Cook's death, a French research expedition was led by de la Pérouse in 1785. Britain's Vancouver Expedition was commissioned in the 1790s to complete Cook's hydrographical work in New Zealand, Australia and Oceania and on the Pacific coast of North America.

resources to continental ends. At the outset, the discernment that extra-European issues might be intrinsically tangled with European interests in diplomacy had, after all, barely existed. Once the Spanish and Portuguese had demarcated their interests to their own satisfaction there was little to concern other European nations. The fate of a French Huguenot settlement in Florida or the flouting of the vague Spanish claims which was implicit in the Roanoke voyages hardly troubled the minds of European diplomats, let alone shaped their negotiations. This situation began to change when English pirates and adventurers countenanced by Elizabeth I began to inflict real damage on the Spanish fleets and colonies. They were soon joined by the Dutch and from this time one of the great themes of the diplomacy of the next century was apparent; as a French minister wrote under Louis XIV, "Trade is the cause of a perpetual combat in war and in peace between the nations of Europe". So much had things changed in two hundred years.

Rulers had, of course, always been concerned with wealth and the opportunity of increasing it. Venice had long defended her commerce by diplomatic means and the English had often safeguarded their cloth exports to Flanders by treaty. It was widely accepted that there was only so much profit to go round and that one country could therefore only gain at the expense of others. But it was a long time before diplomacy had to take account of the pursuit of wealth outside Europe. There was even an attempt to segregate such matters; in 1559 the French and Spanish agreed that what their captains did to

This 16th-century gold medallion, bearing a bust of Queen Elizabeth I of England, commemorates the British victory over the Spanish Armada in 1588.

one another "beyond the line" (which meant at that time west of the Azores, and south of the Tropic of Cancer) should not be taken as a reason for hostility between the two states in Europe.

TRADE WARS

THE CHANGE TO A NEW SET of diplomatic assumptions, if that is the way to put it, began in conflicts over trade with the Spanish Empire. Contemporary thinking took it for granted that in the colonial relationship the interests of the metropolitan power were always paramount. In so far as those interests were economic, settlement colonies were intended to produce, either by exploiting their mineral and natural resources, or by their balance of trade with the mother country, a net advantage to the latter and, if possible, self-sufficiency, while her trading bases gave her the domination of certain areas of international traffic. By 1600 it was clear that claims would be settled by sea-power, and since the defeat of the Armada Spanish sea-power no longer commanded the respect it had done. Essentially, Philip was caught in a dilemma: the dispersal of his effort and interest between Europe – where the struggle with the Valois and Elizabeth, the Dutch Revolt, and the Counter-Reformation all claimed his resources – and the Indies, where safety could have lain only in sea-power and the organization of effective Spanish supply of the colonists' needs. The choice was to try to keep the empire, but to use it to pay for European policies. This was to underrate the difficulties of controlling so huge an empire through sixteenth-century bureaucracy and communications. Nevertheless a huge and complicated system of regular sailings in convoy, the concentration of colonial trade in a few authorized ports and policing by coastguard squadrons were ways in which the Spanish tried to keep the wealth of the Indies to themselves.

It was the Dutch who first made it clear that they were prepared to fight for a share of such prizes and therefore first forced diplomats to turn their attention and skills to regulating matters outside Europe. For the Dutch, predominance in trade overrode other considerations. What they would do for it was made clear from the start of the seventeenth century, in the East Indies, the Caribbean, and Brazil, where they engaged great fleets against the Spanish-Portuguese defence of the world's chief producer of sugar. The last provided their only serious setback, for in 1654 the Portuguese were able to evict the Dutch garrisons and resume control without subsequent challenge.

ANGLO-DUTCH TRADE WARS

The quest for commercial wealth cut across the wishes of the most Protestant of English seventeenth-century governments; England had been an ally of the Dutch rebels in the previous century and Cromwell would have liked nothing better than the leadership of a Protestant alliance against Catholic Spain. Instead he found himself fighting the first of three Anglo-Dutch wars. The first (1652–4) was essentially a trade war. What was at issue was the English decision to restrict imports to England to goods travelling in English ships or those of the country producing the goods. This was a deliberate attempt to encourage English shipping and put it in a position to catch up with the Dutch. It struck at the heart of Dutch prosperity, its European carrying

trade and, in particular, that in Baltic goods. The Commonwealth had a good navy and won. The second round came in 1665, after the Dutch had been further provoked by the English seizure of New Amsterdam. In this war the Dutch had the French and Danes as allies and also had the best of it at sea. At the peace they were therefore able to win an easing of the English restrictions on imports though they left New Amsterdam to the English in exchange for an offshoot of Barbados at Surinam. This was decided by the Treaty of Breda (1667), the first multilateral European peace settlement to say as much about the regulation of extra-European affairs as European. By it France surrendered West Indian islands to England and received in return recognition of her possession of the uninhabited and uninviting but strategically important territory of Acadia. The English

By the late 17th century Amsterdam was the main distribution centre in Europe and most Dutch cities were governed by the wealthiest merchants or by the descendants of great merchant families. This portrait, painted in 1669 by Bartholomeus van der Helst (1613–1670), depicts the Dutch merchant Daniel Bernhard.

t' Fort nieuw Amsterdam op de Manhatans.

had done well; the new Caribbean acquisitions followed in a tradition established under the Commonwealth, when Jamaica had been taken from Spain to be added to the existing plantation colonies.

Cromwell's policies have been seen as a decisive turn towards conscious imperial policy. This may be attributing too much to his vision. The returned Stuarts indeed kept intact most of the "Navigation" system for the protection of shipping and colonial trade, as well as hanging on to Jamaica and continuing to recognize the new importance of the West Indies. Charles II gave a charter to a new company, named after the Hudson Bay, to contest with the French the fur trade of the north and west. He and his in other ways inadequate successor, James II, at least maintained (even if with some setbacks) English naval strength so that it was available to William of Orange in his wars with Louis XIV.

THE ANGLO-FRENCH STRUGGLE

It would be tedious to trace the detailed changes of the century and a half after 1660 when the new imperial emphasis first of

English and then of British diplomacy came to maturity. A brief third Anglo-Dutch war (it had virtually no important consequences) does not really belong to this epoch which is dominated by the long rivalry of England and France. The War of the League of Augsburg (or King William's War, as it was called in America) brought much colonial fighting, but no great changes. The War of the Spanish Succession was very different. It was a world war, the first of the modern era, about the fate of the Spanish Empire as well as about French power. At its close, the British not only won Acadia (henceforth Nova Scotia) and other acquisitions in the western hemisphere from the French, but also the right to supply slaves to the Spanish colonies and to send one ship a year with merchandise to trade with them.

GLOBAL WARFARE

Overseas matters loomed larger and larger in British foreign policy after the War of the Spanish Succession. European considerations mattered less, in spite of the change of dynasty in 1714, when the elector of Hanover became the first king of Great Britain. Though there were some embarrassing moments, British policy remained remarkably consistent, always swinging back to the goals of promoting, sustaining and extending British commerce. Often this was best done by seeking to maintain a general peace, sometimes by diplomatic pressure (as when the Habsburgs were persuaded to withdraw a scheme for an Ostend company to trade with Asia), sometimes by fighting to maintain privileges or strategical advantage.

The importance of war became clearer and clearer. The first time that two European powers ever went to war on a purely non-European issue came in 1739 when the British government began hostilities with

Spain over, in essence, the Spanish right of search in the Caribbean – or, as the Spanish might have put it, over the steps they properly took to secure their empire against abuse of the trading privileges granted in 1713. This was to be remembered as the "War of Jenkins' Ear" – the organ produced in pickle by its owner in the House of Commons, whose sensitive patriotism was inflamed and outraged to hear of the alleged mutilation by a Spanish coastguard. The conflict was soon caught up with the War of the Austrian Succession, and therefore became an Anglo-French struggle. The peace of 1748 did not much change the respective territorial position of the two rivals, nor did it end fighting in North America, where the French appeared to be about to cut off the British settlements for ever from the American west by a chain of forts. The British government sent its first regular contingents to America to meet this danger, but unsuccessfully; only in the Seven Years' War did a British minister grasp that the chance of a final decision in the long duel existed because of France's commitment to her ally Austria in Europe. Once British resources were allocated in accordance with this, sweeping victories in North America and India were followed by others in the Caribbean, some at the expense of

Spain. A British force even seized the Philippines. It was global war.

THE FIRST BRITISH EMPIRE

THE PEACE OF 1763 DID NOT in fact go so far in crippling France and Spain as many Britons had wanted. But it virtually eliminated French competition in North America and India. When it was a question of retaining Canada or Guadeloupe, a sugar-producing island, one consideration in favour of keeping Canada was that competition from increased sugar production within the empire was feared by Caribbean planters already under the British flag. The result was a huge British empire. By 1763, the whole of eastern North America and the Gulf Coast as far west as the mouth of the Mississippi was British. The elimination of French Canada had blown away the threat – or, from the French point of view, the hope – of a French empire of the Mississippi valley, stretching from the St Lawrence to New Orleans, which had been created by the great French explorers of the seventeenth century. Off the continental coast the Bahamas were the northern link of an island chain that ran down through the lesser Antilles to Tobago, and all but enclosed the

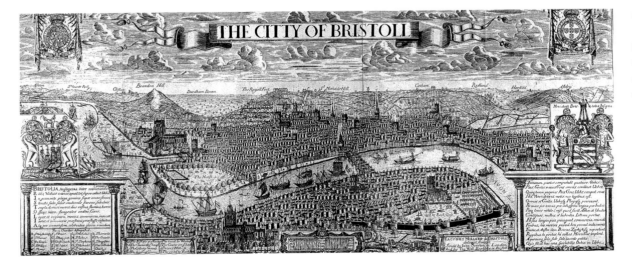

The English city of Bristol, an important port since the 13th century, is shown in this 17th-century engraving.

England's numerous well-protected ports played a key role in its economic growth. This 18th-century painting depicts the bustling docks and quay at the port of Bristol.

Caribbean. Within it, Jamaica, Honduras and the Belize coast were British. In the Peace of 1713, the British had exacted a limited legal right to trade in slaves with the Spanish Empire which they quickly pressed far beyond its intended limits. In Africa there were only a few British posts on the Gold Coast but these were the bases of the huge African slave trade. In Asia the direct government of Bengal was about to provide a start to the territorial phase of British expansion in India.

THE MERCHANT MARINE

British imperial supremacy was based on sea-power. Its ultimate origins could be sought in the ships built by Henry VIII,

among the greatest warships of the age (the *Harry Grâce à Dieu* carried 186 guns), but this early start was neglected under his successors until the reign of Elizabeth I. Her captains, with little financing available either from Crown or commercial investors, built both a fighting tradition and better ships from the profits of operations against the Spanish. Again, there was an ebbing of interest and effort under the early Stuart kings. The royal administration could not afford ships (and paying for new ones was, indeed, one of the causes of the royal taxes Parliament had raged over). It was only under the Commonwealth, ironically, that the serious and continuing interest in naval power which sustained the Royal Navy of the future began. By that time, the connexion between Dutch superiority in merchant shipping and their naval strength had been taken to heart and the upshot was the Navigation Act which provoked the first Anglo-Dutch war. A strong merchant marine provided a nursery of seamen for fighting vessels and the flow of trade whose taxation by customs dues would finance the upkeep of specialized warships. A strong merchant marine could only be built upon carrying the goods of other nations: hence the importance of competing, if necessary by gunfire, and of breaking into such reserved areas as the Spanish American trade.

MARITIME TECHNOLOGY

The machines which were evolved to do the fighting in the competition for trade underwent steady improvement and specialization, but no revolutionary change, between the fifteenth and nineteenth centuries. Once square-rigging and broadside firing had been adopted, the essential shape of vessels was determined, though individual design could still do much to give sailing superiority and the French usually built better ships than Great Britain during the eighteenth-century duel between the two countries. In the sixteenth century, under English influence, ships grew longer in proportion to their beam. The relative height of the forecastle and poop above the deck gradually came down, too, over the whole period. Bronze guns reached a high level of development even in the early seventeenth century; thereafter gunnery changed by improvement in design, accuracy and weight of shot. There were two significant eighteenth-century innovations, the short-range but large-calibre and heavy-shotted iron carronade, which greatly increased the power of even small vessels, and a firing mechanism incorporating a flintlock which made possible more precise control of the guns.

Specialization of function and design between warships and merchant vessels was accepted by the middle of the seventeenth century, though the line was still somewhat blurred by the existence of older vessels and the practice of privateering. This was a way of obtaining naval power on the cheap. In time of war, governments authorized individual private captains or their employers to prey upon enemy shipping, taking profits from the prizes they made. It was a form of regularized piracy and English, Dutch and French privateers all operated at various times with great success against one another's traders. The first great privateering war was that fought unsuccessfully against the English and Dutch under King William by the French.

Other seventeenth-century innovations were tactical and administrative. Signalling became formalized and the first Fighting Instructions were issued to the Royal Navy. Recruitment became more important; the press-gang appeared in England (the French used naval conscription in the maritime provinces). In this way large fleets were manned and it became clear that, given equality of

A commercial port began to develop around the estuary of Plymouth Sound in the 16th century. At the end of the 17th century a military base, Devonport, was founded nearby and by the 18th century the large naval shipyard depicted in this contemporary painting had been established.

skill and the limited damage which could be done even by heavy guns, numbers were always likely to be decisive in the end.

BRITISH SEA-POWER

From the seminal period of development in the seventeenth century there emerged a naval supremacy which was to last over two centuries and underpin a world-wide *pax Britannica*. Dutch competition dropped away as the Republic bent under the strain of defending its independence on land against the French. The important maritime rival of the English was France and here it is possible to see that a decisive point had been passed by the end of King William's reign. By then, the dilemma of being great on land or sea had been decided by the French in favour

of the land. From that time, the promise of a French naval supremacy was never to be revived, though French shipbuilders and captains would still win victories by their skill and courage. The English were not so distracted from oceanic power; they had only to keep their continental allies in the field, not to keep up great armies themselves. But there was a little more to it than a simple concentration of resources. British maritime strategy also evolved in a way very different from that of other sea-powers. Here, the French loss of interest in the navy of Louis XIV is in point, for it came after the English had inflicted a resounding defeat in a fleet action in 1692 which discredited the French admirals. It was the first of many such victories which demonstrated an appreciation of the strategical reality that sea-power was in the end a matter of commanding the surface of the sea so that friendly ships could move on it in safety while those of the enemy could not. The key to this desirable end was the neutralization of the enemy's fleet. So long as it was there, a danger existed. The early defeat of the enemy's fleet in battle therefore became the supreme aim of British naval commanders for a century during which it gave the Royal Navy almost uninterrupted command of the seas and a formidable offensive tradition.

Naval strategy fed imperial enterprise indirectly as well as directly because it made more and more necessary the acquisition of bases from which squadrons could operate. This was particularly important in building the British Empire. In the late eighteenth century, too, that empire was about to undergo the loss of much of its settled territory and this would bring further into relief the way in which European hegemony was, outside the New World, still in 1800 a matter of trading stations, island plantations and bases, and the control of carrying trade, rather than of occupation of large areas.

Stock exchanges were founded in Amsterdam, London, Paris, Hamburg and Frankfurt during the 17th century. The Amsterdam Exchange is seen in this painting by Emmanuel de Witte (1617–1692).

A WORLD ECONOMY IN THE MAKING

Less than three centuries of even a limited form of imperialism revolutionized the world economy. Before 1500, there had been hundreds of more or less self-supporting and self-contained economies, some of them linked by trade. The Americas and Africa were almost, Australasia entirely, unknown to Europe, communication within them was tiny in proportion to their huge extent, and there was a thin flow of luxury trade from Asia to Europe. By 1800, a worldwide network of exchange had appeared. Even Japan was a part of it and central Africa, though still mysterious and unknown, was linked to it through slaving and the Arabs. Its first two striking adumbrations had been the diversion of Asian trade with Europe to the sea routes dominated by the Portuguese and the flow of bullion from America to Europe. Without that stream, above all of silver, there could hardly have been a trade with Asia for there

Precious metals extracted from Peruvian mines, such as the one shown in this 18th-century illustration, were highly sought after and quickly made an impact on the European economy. Other products, including foodstuffs, livestock, plants and minerals, were slowly introduced to early modern Europe, with varying degrees of success.

was almost nothing produced in Europe that Asia wanted. This may have been the main importance of the bullion from the Americas, whose flow reached its peak at the end of the sixteenth century and in the early decades of the next.

Although a new abundance of precious metals was the first and most dramatically obvious economic effect of Europe's new interplay with Asia and America, it was less important than the general growth of trade, of which slaves from Africa for the Caribbean and Brazil formed a part. The slave-ships usually made their voyage back to Europe from the Americas loaded with the colonial

This illustration shows the boiling of bamboo shoots in 16th-century China to produce paper paste for export to Europe. The aim of trade with Asia was not to find new markets for European goods, but to supply Europe with luxury products. Except for arms and munitions, the only European commodity wanted in the East was silver.

At the beginning of the 16th century, tobacco was grown in medicinal gardens in Europe. By the 1850s the amount of tobacco imported from North America had exceeded that produced in Europe. This engraving of a tobacco plant dates from the late 18th century.

Tea was first brought to Europe from China by the Dutch East India Company in 1609. In 1646 the English East India Company began to import it and the first shop to specialize in retailing tea was probably Twinings, which opened in London in 1713. This painting, dating from 1764, portrays a group of French aristocrats enjoying English-style tea in the Palais du Temple in Paris.

produce which more and more became a necessity to Europe. In Europe, first Amsterdam and then London surpassed Antwerp as international ports, in large measure because of the huge growth of the re-export trade in colonial goods which were carried by Dutch and English ships. Around these central flows of trade there proliferated branches and sub-branches which led to further specializations and ramifications. Shipbuilding, textiles and, later, financial services such as insurance all prospered together, sharing in the consequences of a huge expansion in sheer volume. Eastern trade in the second half of the eighteenth century made up a quarter of the whole of Dutch external commerce and during that century the number of ships sent out by the East India Company from London went up threefold. These ships, moreover, thanks to improvements in design, carried more and were worked by fewer men than those of earlier times.

CHANGES IN EUROPEAN LIFESTYLE

The material consequences of Europe's new involvement with the world are much easier to measure than some of the others. European diet remains one of the most varied in the world and this came about in the early modern age. The coming of tobacco, coffee, tea and sugar alone brought about a revolution in taste, habit and housekeeping. The potato was to change the lives of many countries by sustaining much larger populations than its predecessors. Scores of drugs were added to the European pharmacopoeia, mainly from Asia.

INTELLECTUAL IMPACT

Beyond the material effects of Europe's colonialization it is harder to proceed. The interplay of new knowledge of the world with European mentality is especially hard to pin down. Minds were changing, as the great increase in the numbers of books about discoveries and voyages in both East and West showed as early as the sixteenth century. Oriental studies may be said to have been founded as a science in the seventeenth century, though Europeans only begin to show the impact of knowledge of the anthropologies of other people towards its close. Such developments were intensified in the unrolling of their effects by the fact that they took place in an age of printing, too, and this makes the novelty of interest in the world outside Europe hard to evaluate. By the early eighteenth century, though, there were signs of an important intellectual impact at a deep level. Idyllic descriptions of savages who lived moral lives without the help of Christianity provoked reflexion; an English philosopher, John Locke, used the evidence of other continents to show that human beings did not share any God-given innate ideas. In particular, China furnished examples for speculation on the relativity of social institutions, while the penetration of Chinese literature (much aided by the studies of the Jesuits) revealed a chronology whose length made nonsense of traditional calculations of the date of the Flood described in the Bible as the second beginning of humanity.

As its products became more easily available, China also provoked in Europe an eighteenth-century craze for oriental styles in furniture, porcelain and dress. As an artistic and intellectual influence this has remained more obvious than the deeper perspective given to the observation of European life by an awareness of different civilizations with different standards elsewhere. But while such comparisons may have had some disquieting aspects, revealing that Europe had, perhaps, less to be proud of in its attitude to other

Painted in 1793, this watercolour shows the Chinese emperor Ts'ien-lung and his entourage at a reception ceremony for the first British ambassador to China, Lord Macartney.

religions than China, there were still others suggested by exploits such as those of the conquistadores which fed Europeans' notions of their superiority.

THE IMPACT OF EUROPE ON THE WORLD

THE IMPACT OF EUROPE on the world is no easier to encapsulate in a few simple formulae than that of the world upon Europe, but it is, in some of its manifestations at least, at times more dramatically obvious. It is an appalling fact that almost nowhere in the world can the inhabitants of non-European countries be shown to have benefited materially from the first phase of Europe's expansion; far from it, they often suffered terribly. Yet this was not always something for which blame attaches to the Europeans – unless they should be blamed for being there at all. In an age with no knowledge of infectious disease beyond the most elementary, the devastating impact of smallpox or other diseases brought from Europe to the Americas could not have been anticipated. But it was disastrous. It has been calculated that the population of Mexico fell by three-quarters in the sixteenth century; that of some Caribbean islands was wiped out altogether.

Such facts as the ruthless exploitation of those who survived, on the other hand, whose labour was so much more valuable after this demographic collapse, are a different matter. Here is expressed that *leitmotiv* of subjection and domination which runs through well-nigh every instance of Europe's early impact on the rest of the world. Different colonial environments and different European traditions present gradations of oppression and exploitation. Not all colonial societies were based on the same extremes of brutality and horror. But all were tainted. The wealth of the United Provinces and its magnificent seventeenth-century civilization were fed by roots which, at least in the spice islands and Indonesia, lay in bloody ground. Long before expansion in North America went west of the Alleghenies, the brief good relations of the first English settlers of Virginia with the Native North Americans had soured and extermination and eviction had begun. Though the populations of Spanish America had been in some measure protected by the state from the worst abuses of the *encomienda* system, they had for the most part been reduced to peonage, while determined efforts were made (for the highest motives) to destroy their culture. In South Africa the fate of the Hottentot and in Australia that of the Aborigine would repeat the lesson that European culture could devastate those whom it touched, unless they had the protection of old and advanced civilizations such as those of India or China. Even in those great countries, much damage would be done, nor would they be able to resist the Europeans once they decided to bring sufficient force to bear. But it was the settled colonies that showed most clearly the pattern of domination.

THE COSTS OF SLAVERY

THE PROSPERITY OF MANY European colonies long depended on the African slave trade, whose economic importance has already been touched upon. Since the eighteenth century it has obsessed critics who have seen in it the most brutal example of the inhumanity of man to man, whether that of white to black, of European to non-European, or of capitalist to labourer. It has properly dominated much of the historiography of Europe's expansion and American civilization, for it was a major fact in both. Less usefully, it has, because of its importance in shaping so much of the New World, diverted attention from other forms of slavery at other times – or even alternative fates to slavery, such as the extermination, intentional or unintentional, which overtook other peoples.

Outlets in the New World settler colonies were to dominate the direction of the slave trade until its abolition in the nineteenth century. First in the Caribbean islands and then on the American mainland, the slavers found their most reliable customers. The Portuguese who had first dominated the trade were soon elbowed out by the Dutch and then by Elizabeth I's "sea-dogs". Meanwhile, Portuguese captains turned to importing slaves to Brazil instead as the sixteenth century went on. Early in the seventeenth century the Dutch founded a company to ensure a regular supply of slaves to the West Indies, but by 1700 their lead had been overtaken by French and English slavers who had established their own posts on the "slave coast" of Africa. Altogether, their efforts sent between nine and ten millions of black slaves to the western hemisphere, 80 per cent of them after 1700. The eighteenth century saw the greatest prosperity of the trade; some six million slaves were shipped then. European ports like Bristol and Nantes built a new age of commercial wealth on slaving. New lands were opened as black slave labour made it possible to work them. Larger-scale production of new crops brought, in turn, great changes in European demand, manufacturing and trading patterns. Racially, too, we still live with the results.

CRUELTY AND DESTRUCTION

What has disappeared and can now never be measured is the human misery involved, not merely in physical hardship (a black man

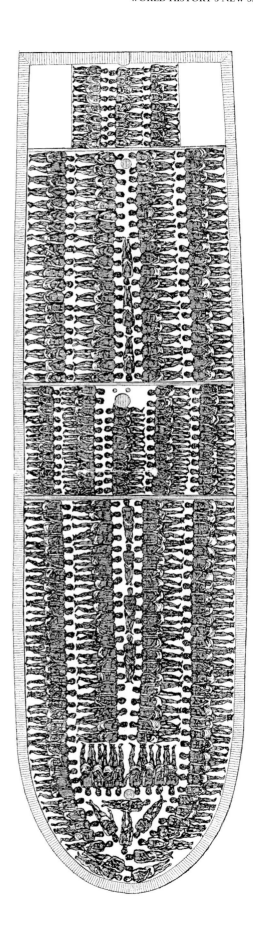

This plan of an 18th-century slave ship shows how tightly African slaves were packed into the vessel's hull in order to maximize the numbers the ship could carry. Conditions during the long journeys undertaken by such ships were horrendous and death rates of more than 40 per cent among the slaves were not uncommon.

Slave merchants are shown negotiating the sale of two black slaves in Gorée, in Senegal, Africa, in an illustration dated 1796.

might live only a few years on a West Indian plantation even if he survived the horrible conditions of the voyage) but in the psychological and emotional tragedies of this huge migration. Historians still debate whether slavery "civilized" blacks in the Americas by bringing them into contact, willy-nilly, with higher civilizations, or whether it retarded them in quasi-infantile dependence. The question seems as insoluble as the degree of cruelty involved is incalculable; on the one hand is the evidence of the fetters and the whipping-block, on the other the reflexion that these were commonplaces of European life too, and that, a priori, self-interest should have prompted the planters to care for their investment. That it did not always do so, slave rebellions showed. Such resistance, though, was infrequent, a fact which also bears reflexion. It is unlikely that the debate will end.

Estimates of the almost unrecorded damage done in Africa are even harder to arrive at, for the evidence is even more subject to conjecture. The obvious demographic loss may (as some historians have hazarded) be balanced against the introduction to Africa of new foodstuffs from America. Conceivably, such by-products of a European contact determined by the hunt for slaves actually led to population growth, but the hypothesis can hardly be weighed against the equally immeasurable effects of imported disease.

EUROPEAN ACCEPTANCE OF THE SLAVE TRADE

It is notable that the African slave trade for a long time awoke no misgivings such as those which had been shown by Spanish churchmen in defence of the American Indians, and the arguments with which some Christians actually resisted the restriction of this traffic still retain a certain gruesome fascination. Feelings of responsibility and guilt began to emerge widely only in the eighteenth century and mainly in France and England. One expression of it was the British acquisition of another dependency in 1787, Sierra Leone, soon adopted by philanthropists as a refuge for African slaves freed in England. Once combined with a favourable political and economic conjuncture, the current of public feeling educated by humanitarian thought would destroy the slave trade and, in the European world, slavery. But that is part of a different story. In the unfolding of European world power, slavery was a huge social and economic fact. It was also to become a great mythical one, symbolizing at its harshest the triumph of force and cupidity over humanity. Sadly, it was also only the outstanding expression of a general dominance by force of advanced societies over weaker ones.

French law on the treatment of slaves

Art. 16: We forbid slaves belonging to different masters to gather together, by day or by night, under pain of corporal punishment which will be no less than flogging or a fleur-de-lis (branding on the back); and in the case of frequent repetition of the offence and other aggravating circumstances, the slave can be condemned to death, which we leave to the discretion of the judges. We entrust all our subjects with the persecution of those who violate the law, of detaining them and taking them to prison, although they are not officials and although there is no decree of arrest.

Art. 33: Any slave who hits his master, or his master's wife, his mistress or the husband of his mistress, or their children causing bruising or bloodshed, will be punished with death.

Art. 38: A fugitive slave who has been on the run for a month from the day of being reported to the court by his master, will have his ears cut off and will be marked by a fleur-de-lis on his shoulder; and if he repeats the offence from the day of being reported he will have the back of his knees cut and will be marked with a fleur-de-lis on the other shoulder; on the third time he will be punished with death.

Art. 44: We decree that slaves are furniture, and as such they become property, that consequently they cannot be leased, that they are divided into equal parts amongst the co-inheritors, without testimonial preferences nor right of primogeniture, that they are not subject to the usual widow's pension, to a feudal and dependent's pension, to feudal rights, to the formalities of decrees nor to the reductions of the four fifths, in the case of settlements of any last will and testament.

Extracts from the code of law on the policy of the Islands of the Archipelago, Versailles, March 1685. From *Recueil général des anciennes lois françaises* by Isambert.

CATHOLIC MISSIONARIES

Some Europeans recognized the inhuman nature of the slave trade but none the less believed that any evil was outweighed by what they offered to the rest of the world, above all, by the bringing of Christianity. It was a bull of Paul III, the pope who summoned the Council of Trent, which proclaimed that "the Indians are truly men and … are not only capable of understanding the Catholic faith but according to our information, they desire exceedingly to receive it". Such optimism was not merely an expression of the Counter-Reformation spirit, for the missionary impulse had been there from the start in the Spanish and Portuguese possessions. Jesuit missionary work began in Goa in 1542 and radiated from there all over the Indian Ocean and Southeast Asia and even reached Japan. Like the other Catholic powers, the French, too, emphasized missionary work, even in areas where France was not herself economically or politically involved. A new vigour was none the less given to missionary enterprise in the sixteenth and seventeenth centuries and may be acknowledged as one invigorating effect of the Counter-Reformation. Formally at least, Roman Christianity took in more converts and greater tracts of territory in the sixteenth century than in any earlier. What this really meant is harder to assess, but what little protection the native had was often only provided by the Roman Catholic Church, whose theologians kept alive the only notion of trusteeship towards subject peoples which existed in early imperial theory.

PROTESTANT MISSIONARIES

Protestantism lagged far behind Catholicism in concern about the natives of settlement

Christian missionary activity in the European colonies

By the beginning of the 19th century, Roman Catholic missions were firmly established in most of the French, Spanish and Portuguese colonies in Asia and Africa. Protestant missionary activity had been less common until this period, when British colonial expansion (and the influence of Evangelical Revivalism) resulted in the presence of Protestant missionaries in every part of the British Empire.

The success rates of European missionaries in the colonies were very mixed. Islam, Hinduism, Buddhism and Confucianism proved too highly resistant to the Christian creeds, unlike many native African religions.

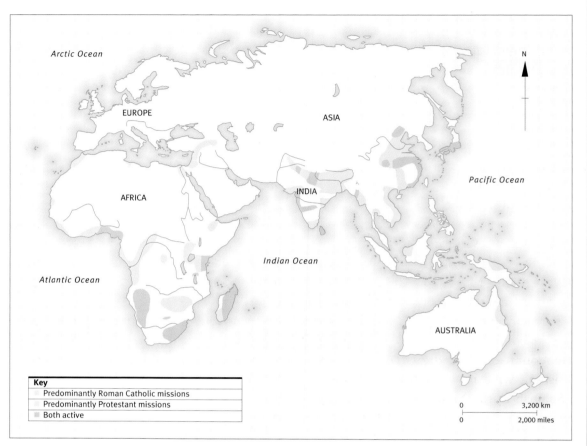

This map shows areas of colonial missionary activity in 19th-century Africa and Asia.

colonies, as it did in missionary work. The Dutch hardly did anything and the English American colonists not only failed to convert, but actually enslaved some of their Native North American neighbours (the Quakers of Pennsylvania were laudable exceptions). The origins of the great Anglo-Saxon overseas missionary movements are not to be detected until the end of the seventeenth century. Furthermore, even in the gift of the Gospel to the world when it came there lay a tragic ambiguity. It, too, was a European export of enormously corrosive potential, challenging and undermining traditional structures and ideas, threatening social authority, legal and moral institutions, family and marriage

patterns. The missionaries, often in spite of themselves, became instruments of the process of domination and subjugation which runs through the story of Europe's intercourse with the rest of the globe.

EUROPEAN TRANSPLANTS

Perhaps there was nothing Europeans brought with them which would not in the end turn out to be a threat, or at least double-edged. The food plants which the Portuguese carried from America to Africa in the sixteenth century – these included cassava, sweet potatoes and maize – may have improved African diet, but (it has been argued) may also have provoked population growth which led to social disruption and upheaval. Plants taken to the Americas, on the other hand, founded new industries which then created a demand for slaves; coffee and sugar were commodities of this sort. Further north, wheat-growing by British settlers did not require slaves, but intensified the demand for land and added to the pressures driving the colonists into the ancestral hunting-grounds of the Indians, whom they ruthlessly pushed out of the way.

The lives of generations unborn when such transplants were first made were to be shaped by them, and a longer perspective than one confined by 1800 is helpful here. Wheat was, after all, ultimately to make the western hemisphere the granary of European cities; in our own century even Russia and Asian countries have drawn on it. A still-flourishing wine industry was implanted by the Spanish in the Madeiras and America as early as the sixteenth century. When bananas were established in Jamaica, coffee in Java and tea in Ceylon, the groundwork was laid of much future politics. All such changes, moreover, were in the nineteenth century complicated by variations in demand, as industrialization increased the demand for old staples such as cotton (in 1760 England imported two and a half million pounds of raw cotton – in 1837 the figure was three hundred and sixty million) and sometimes created new ones; it was a consequence of this that rubber was successfully transplanted from South America to Malaya, a change fraught with great strategic significance for the future.

In the African Cape of Good Hope, the Dutch East India Company discouraged export, considering the region to be a strategic base and a centre for the supply of food to its traders rather than a colony. This painting shows a Boer family's house in the north of the Cape.

ECOLOGICAL CHANGE

The scope of such implications for the future in the early centuries of European hegemony will appear sufficiently in what follows. Here it is only important to note one more, often-repeated, characteristic of this pattern, its unplanned, casual nature. It was the amalgam of many individual decisions by compara-tively few men. Even their most innocent innovations could have explosive conse-quences. It is worth recalling that it was the importation of a couple of dozen rabbits in 1859 which led to the devastation of much of rural Australia by millions of them within a few decades. Similarly, but on a smaller scale, Bermuda was to be plagued with English toads.

Conscious animal importations, though, were even more important (the first response to the Australian rabbit scourge was to send for English stoats and weasels; a better answer had to wait for myxomatosis). Almost the entire menagerie of European domesticated animals was settled in the Americas by 1800. The most important were cattle and horses. Between them they would revolutionize the

The European-style buildings in this view of 18th-century Canton in southern China are testimony to the presence of French, North American, English and Dutch commercial companies.

life of the Plains Indians; later, after the coming of refrigerated ships, they were to make South America a great meat exporter just as Australasia was to be made one by the introduction of sheep the English had themselves imported originally from Spain. And, of course, the Europeans brought human bloodstock, too. Like the British in America, the Dutch for a long time did not encourage the mixing of races. Yet in Latin America, Goa and Portuguese Africa the effects were profound. So, in an entirely different and negative way, were they in British North America, where racial intermarriage was not significant and the near-exact coincidence of colour and legally servile status bequeathed an enormous legacy of political, economic, social and cultural problems to the future.

PROBLEMS OF IMPERIAL GOVERNMENT

The creation of large colonial populations shaped the future map, but also presented problems of government. The British colonies

nearly always had some form of representative institution which reflected parliamentary tradition and practice while France, Portugal and Spain all followed a straightforward authoritarian and monarchical institutional system. None of them envisaged any sort of independence for their colonists, nor any need to safeguard their interests against those of the mother country, whether these were conceived as paramount or complementary. This would in the end cause trouble and by 1763 there were signs at least in the British North American colonies that it might be on lines reminiscent of seventeenth-century England's struggles between Crown and Parliament. And in their struggles with other nations, even when their governments were not formally at war with them, the colonists always showed a lively sense of their own interests. Even when Dutch and English were formally allied against France their sailors and traders would fight one another "beyond the line".

Problems of imperial government in the eighteenth century were, though, largely a matter of the western hemisphere. That was

The English explorer Captain James Cook is portrayed in this 18th-century painting. On his first voyage, Cook left Tahiti to travel round New Zealand and chart eastern Australia. His second journey began in 1772 and crossed the Atlantic and Pacific oceans, with four scouting expeditions below 60° latitude south. The third trip completed charts from the Bering Strait to California; on this final trip Cook aimed to discover the elusive Northwest Passage (a long-sought sea passage along the northern coast of North America), but he was killed in Hawaii in 1779.

where the settlers had gone. Elsewhere in the world in 1800, even in India, trade still mattered more than possession and many important areas had still to feel the full impact of Europe. As late as 1789 the East India Company was sending only twenty-one ships in the year to Canton; the Dutch were allowed two a year to Japan. Central Asia was at that date still only approachable by the long land routes used in the days of Chinghis Khan and the Russians were still far from exercising effective influence over the hinterland. Africa was protected by climate and disease. Discovery and exploration still had to complete that continent's map before European hegemony could become a reality.

EUROPEANS REACH AUSTRALIA

In the Pacific and "South Seas", things were moving faster. Dampier's voyage of 1699 had opened a century of exploration which added Australasia, the last unknown continent, to the map. In the north, the existence of the Bering Straits had been demonstrated by

The last discoveries

During the 17th and 18th centuries, the discovery of new lands continued to be a major preoccupation for the European powers; scouting expeditions multiplied and a large number of exciting new finds were made. Although the search for wealth and power, as well as evangelizing zeal, continued to play an important role, other more concrete reasons for exploration emerged during this period, such as trade and scientific research. Leading explorers also had better technical, nautical and financial backing.

The Pacific was one of the main objectives of this continual discovery effort. In 1605 the Portuguese navigator Pedro Fernández de Quirós began a voyage to the Pacific which would take him to the New Hebrides. The Spaniard Diego de Prados and his colleague Luis Vaez de Torres continued the search and touched the Australian mainland at Cape York. In 1642, a Dutch expedition, led by Abel Tasman, sailed around the Australian coast and discovered Tasmania and New Zealand. Another Dutchman, Jacob Roggeveen, discovered Easter Island in 1721 on a round-the-world voyage from Brazil. In the late 18th century, England sent two teams to Australia to improve nautical charts: John Byron (from 1764 to 1766) and Samuel Wallis and Philip Carteret (from 1766 to 1768) charted the positions of several islands.

This illustration shows Queen Oberea of Tahiti in conversation with the newly arrived Captain Samuel Wallis (1728–1795), who discovered Tahiti and the Wallis Islands during his circumnavigation of the globe from 1766 to 1768.

1730. The voyages of Bougainville and Cook, in the 1760s and 1770s, added Tahiti, Samoa, eastern Australia, Hawaii and New Zealand to the last New World to be opened. Cook even penetrated the Antarctic Circle. In 1788 the first cargo of convicts, 717 of them, was landed in New South Wales. British judges were calling into existence a new penal world to redress the balance of the old, since the American colonies were now unavailable for dumping English undesirables, and were incidentally founding another new nation. More important still, a few years later the first sheep arrived and so was founded the industry to ensure that nation's future. Along with animals, adventurers and ne'er-do-wells there came to the South Pacific, also, the Gospel. In 1797 the first missionaries arrived in Tahiti. With them, the blessings of European civilization may be reckoned at last to have appeared, at least in embryonic form, in every part of the habitable world.

This notice board, promising equal justice to blacks and whites alike, was addressed to the Aboriginal population of Van Diemen's Land (Tasmania), Australia, c.1828. In spite of such assurances, the British governor of the island, Sir George Arthur (1785–1854), actually tried (but failed) to restrict the Aborigines to the southeastern peninsula behind a "Black Line". By the second half of the 19th century, Tasmania's Aboriginal population had been practically wiped out.

Time chart (1490–1795)

1492
Christopher Columbus'
first voyage

Cabral discovers Brazil

1508
Treaty of Cambrai

1512
Council of Lateran

1517
The Portuguese
reach Canton

1521
Diet of Worms
Luther is excommunicated

1500

1510

1520

1498
Vasco da Gama
reaches Calcutta

This painting, from the school of
Hans Holbein the Younger, depicts
Sir Thomas More (1478–1535), the
English Catholic humanist, states-
man and author of *Utopia* (1516).

Sir Thomas More

1519
Charles V
becomes Holy
Roman Emperor

1555
Peace of
Augsburg

1563
Final session of the
Council of Trent

1572
St Bartholomew's
Day massacre

1560

1570

1580

Elizabeth I, Queen of England from 1558
until 1603, maintained the unity of her
realm in the face of Spanish attacks and
threats to her own life by Catholic
supporters of her cousin Mary Stuart.

Queen Elizabeth I of England

This illustration, dated 1580–1583,
shows a galleon equipped with guns.
The possession of armed warships such
as this enabled Europeans to trade with
and colonize regions all over the world.

16th-century European galleon

1619
The Dutch found
Batavia

1626
The Dutch found
New Amsterdam

The English
found Boston

1620

1630

1640

1618
Thirty Years' War starts

1638
Portuguese expelled
from Japan

1644
Chinese Ch
Dynasty be

This statue dates from 1782 and
represents the Russian tsar Peter the
Great (1672–1725) looking out over
St Petersburg, his capital city and the
symbol of his drive to westernize Russia.

Statue of Peter the Great

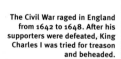

The Civil War raged in England
from 1642 to 1648. After his
supporters were defeated, King
Charles I was tried for treason
and beheaded.

King Charles I of England

1701
Start of the War of
Succession in Spain

1680

1690

1700

1683
John III of Poland defeats
Turks in Vienna

1688
England's "Glorious
Revolution"

Robert Clive meets the nawab
(prince) of Bengal's General Mir Jafar
after the Battle of Plassey in 1757.
The British victory led to their
acquisition of Bengal – they gave
Jafar the defeated nawab's throne.

Robert Clive in India

1759
The British
conquer
Quebec

1762–1796
Catherine the
Great is Empress
of Russia

1738
Treaty of Vienna ends
War of Polish Succession

1740

1750

1760

1748
Treaty of
Aix-la-Chapelle

1756–1763
The Seven Years' War
between England
and France

1529
The Cambrai
Peace Treaty

1531
Pizarro
conquers Peru

The Society of Jesus
receives papal approval

1545
First session of
Council of Trent

1547–1584
Reign of Ivan the
Terrible of Russia

1530 1540 1550

Henry VIII of England (1491–1547)
renounced his subordination to the
Catholic Church of Rome in order to
establish his leadership of the church
in England.

King Henry VIII

The Cathedral of St Basil the
Blessed was built outside the
Kremlin in Moscow in 1555–1560,
after the victory of Kazan, which
ended the long Mongolian rule.

Cathedral of St Basil, Moscow

1587
Foundation
of Virginia

1588
The English defeat the
Spanish Armada

1608
Quebec is founded

1590 1600 1610

1598
Edict of Nantes

1602
The Dutch East India
Company is founded

The Congress of Münster of 15 May 1648, a
scene from which is depicted here, was one of two
parallel conferences that marked the start of the
European peace process to end the Thirty Years'
War, which had been fought across Europe.

Congress of Münster

Restoration of
Charles II in England

1666
Académie des Sciences
founded in Paris

1650 1660 1670

1652
Start of the first
Anglo-Dutch war

1665
Start of second
Anglo-Dutch war

1672
Start of third
Anglo-Dutch war

King Louis XIV of France
(1638– 1715), saw himself as a
role model for Europe's absolute
monarchs. "L'état c'est moi," he
once declared – "I am the state."

Louis XIV of France

1732
British colony of
Georgia is founded

1714
Peace of Utrecht

1710 1720 1730

1718
New Orleans is founded

Savoy is granted Sardinia
in exchange for Sicily

This contemporary print represents
the first partition of Poland in 1772.
The monarchs of Russia, Prussia and
Austria, who shared between them
about a third of Poland's territory,
are shown dividing the spoils.

First partition of Poland

1768
Captain Cook's
first voyage

1740–1786
Reign of Frederick
II of Prussia

1774–1793
Reign of Louis
XVI of France

1770 1780 1790

1764
Hargreaves
invents the
spinning-jenny

1769
Watt patents
the steam-
engine condenser

1773
Pugachev leads a
rebellion in Russia

VOLUME 6 *Chapters and contents*

Chapter 1

A New Kind of Society: Early Modern Europe

Chapter 2

Authority and its Challengers

Chapter 3

The New World of Great Powers

Chapter 4

Europe's Assault on the World

Chapter 5

World History's New Shape

SERIES CONTENTS

INDEX

Page references to main text in roman, to box text in **bold** and to captions in *italic*.

ACKNOWLEDGMENTS

The publishers wish to thank the following for their kind permission to reproduce the illustrations in this book:

KEY

b bottom; **c** centre; **t** top; **l** left; **r** right
AGE: A.G.E. Fotostock
AISA: Archivo Iconografico SA
AKG: AKG London
BAL: Bridgeman Art Library
BL: British Library, London
BM: British Museum, London
BN: Bibliothèque Nationale, Paris
BNM: Biblioteca Nacional, Madrid
BPK: Bildarchiv Preussischer Kulturbesitz, Berlin
DBP: Duncan Baird Publishers
ET: e.t. Archive
KM: Kunsthistorisches Museum, Vienna
MP: Museo del Prado, Madrid
NG: National Gallery, London
NMM: National Maritime Museum, London
NPG: National Portrait Gallery, London
ON: Osterreichischen Nationalbibliothek, Vienna
RMN: Réunion des Musées Nationaux, Paris
SHMM: State Historical Museum, Moscow
SMPK: Staatliche Museen zu Berlin-Preussischer Kulturbesitz
V&A: By courtesy of the board of trustees of the Victoria & Albert Museum, London
WFA: Werner Forman Archive

Front cover: BAL / NG
3 BPK / SMPK / Gemäldegalerie, Berlin
7 Royal Geographic Society, London (Mr.264 H.9)
8 BAL / Lauros-Giraudon / Musée du Ranquet, Clermont-Ferrand
9 MP
10 BAL / Koninklijk Kabinet von Schilderijen Mauritshuis, The Hague
11 BAL / Giraudon / Louvre, Paris
14 Scala / Museo di Firenze com'era, Florence
15t BAL / Národní Galerie, Prague
15b BAL / BL (Add.24098, f.25v)
16 ET / Bibliothèque de L'Ecouen
17 NG
18 KM
19 AISA / Musée Carnavalet, Paris
20 MP
21 BPK / Jörg P. Anders / Staatliche Museen zu Berlin
22 Oronoz / BNM
23 Museo de América, Madrid
24 AKG London / Staatliche Kupferstich-Kabinett, Dresden
25 ET / Frederiksborg Castle, Denmark
26 BAL / Science Museum, London
27 Scala / Pushkin Museum, Moscow
28 RMN / Gérard Blot / Louvre, Paris
29 BM
30 MP

31 RMN / Louvre, Paris
32 BAL / Guildhall Art Library, Corporation of London
33 MP
34 BPK / SMPK / Gemäldegalerie, Berlin
35 Oronoz / Musée des Beaux Arts, Rouen
37 BAL / Wallace Collection, London
38 RMN / Louvre, Paris
39 Scala / Palazzo Vecchio, Florence
40 Giraudon / Bibliothèque de L'Arsenal, Paris
41 ET / Musée de Versailles
42 Lauros-Giraudon / Archives Nationales, Paris
43 NG
44 NG
45t Scala / Galleria degli Uffizi, Florence
45b RMN / Louvre, Paris
46 Scala / Galleria degli Uffizi, Florence
48 BAL / Giraudon / BN
49 BN
50t BAL / National Gallery of Scotland, Edinburgh
50b Oronoz / Musée de l'Histoire, Geneva
51 BAL / Bible Society, London
52 Scala / Galleria Nazionale d'Arte Antica, Rome
53t NPG
53b MP
54 Oronoz
56 RMN / Jean Schormans / Louvre, Paris
57t Oronoz / Catedral de Toledo
57b Oronoz / Coleccion Uria, Azcoitia, Guipuzcoa
58 BAL / Index / Museo Lazaro Galdiano, Madrid
60 BAL / Roy Miles Gallery, London
61 AKG / Maximilian Foundation, Munich
62 NPG
63 BM
64 BAL / The Trustees of the Weston Park Foundation
65 BAL / Giraudon / Château de Versailles
66 BAL / Philip Mould Historical Portraits Ltd, London
67 NG
68 RMN / Musée des Granges de Port Royal
69 AKG
70 BM
72 Oronoz / Embajada Francesa, Madrid
73 MP
74t ET / SHMM
74b AISA
75 Oronoz
77 AISA
78 Oronoz / Academia de Bellas Artes de San Fernando, Madrid
80 Musées Royaux des Beaux-Arts de Belgique, Brussels
81 ON (Cod. 1875, f.41v)
82 MP
83 RMN / Hervé Lewandowski / Louvre, Paris
84 BAL / KM
85 Oronoz / Biblioteca del Monasterio de El Escorial, Madrid

86 NG
87 BN
89 ET / BN
90 AISA / Musée de Versailles
91 Oronoz / Biblioteca del Monasterio de El Escorial, Madrid
92 MP
93 BAL / BL (Add.33733, f.9)
94 Giraudon / BAL / NG
95 BN (Turk. 524, f.218v)
96t BAL / Stapleton Collection, London
96b AISA / Historisches Museum der Stadt, Vienna
98t AISA / Musée de Versailles
99t AISA / Muzeum Narodowe, Warsaw
99b AISA / Gallerie degli Uffizi, Florence
100 National Museum, Copenhagen / Niels Elswing
101 AISA
102 AISA / BN
103 V&A
105 TRIP / M. Jenkin
106t BAL / Tretyakov Gallery, Moscow
106b BN
108t Novosti, London
108b BAL / Stapleton Collection, London
109 BAL / Private Collection
110 AISA / Tretyakov Gallery, Moscow
111 AISA / Tretyakov Gallery, Moscow
112 John Massey Stewart / Tretyakov Gallery, Moscow
113t ET / SHMM
113b AISA
114 AISA / SHMM
115 Novosti, London
116 AISA
117 Lauros-Giraudon
118 OM
121 AKG
122 Oronoz / Musée des Beaux-Arts, Rouen
123 BN
124 BAL / NMM
125 BAL / Musei e Gallerie Pontificie, Vatican City
127 AKG
129 Oronoz / BNM
130 WFA / BM
131 AKG
132 BAL / Johnny Van Haeften Gallery, London
133 Rijksmuseum, Amsterdam
134 BAL / V&A
136 NPG
139 BNM (Ms 50, f.371)
140t BNM (Ms 50, f.484)
140b Museo de América, Madrid
142 Oronoz / BNM
143 Oronoz / Archivo General de las Indias, Seville
144 NPG
145 BN
146 DBP
148 AISA / BNM
149 North Wind Picture Archives

150 BM
151 BM
153 ET
156 Museo Municipal, Madrid
157 BAL / National Library of Australia, Canberra
158 Michael Holford / BM
159 Museum Boymans-Van Beuningen, Rotterdam
160 North Wind Picture Archives
161 BAL / City of Bristol Museum and Art Gallery
162 BAL / City of Bristol Museum and Art Gallery
163 NMM
164 Museum Boymans-Van Beuningen, Rotterdam / Willem van der Vorm Foundation
165t Oronoz / Biblioteca del Palacio Real, Madrid
165b BN
166t Oronoz / Biblioteca del Palacio Real, Madrid
166b RMN / Gérard Blot / Musée de Versailles
167 BM
169 North Wind Picture Archives
170 AISA / Union des Arts Décoratifs, Paris
173 BM
174-75 Maritiem Museum, Rotterdam
176 NMM
177 BAL / BM
179 Tasmanian Museum & Art Gallery, Hobart

MAPS

Maps copyright © 1998 Debate pages 13, 96, 107
Maps copyright © 1998 Helicon/Debate pages 55, 88, 126, 128, 138, 141, 147, 155, 172

TEXT CREDITS

The publishers wish to thank the following for their kind permission to reproduce the translations and copyright material in this book. Every effort has been made to trace copyright owners, but if anyone has been omitted we apologize and will, if informed, make corrections in any future edition.

p.39 extract from *The Prince* by Niccolò Machiavelli, translated by George Bull (Penguin Classics 1961, Revised edition 1975) copyright © George Bull, 1961, 1975, 1981. Reproduced by permission of Penguin Books Ltd.